Hear the Wind, See the Wind

Hear the Wind, See the Wind

Stefan C. Nadzo
Nancy R. Nadzo

Also by Stefan C. Nadzo
There Is A Way
Take Off Your Shoes
Being Who You Are

Copyright 1987 by Stefan C. Nadzo and Nancy R. Nadzo

All Rights Reserved

Library of Congress Catalog Card Number: 87-82954
International Standard Book Number: 0-937226-03-3

Cover art and book design by Nancy R. Nadzo

Printed in offset by Pioneer Print of Ellsworth, Maine

Manufactured in the United States of America

Published by EDEN'S WORK

Franklin, Maine 04634

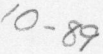

Consider this. The Spirit of God is likened to the wind which we cannot see, and which we know only by its effects. And so we worship Jesus of Nazareth and others like him in the flesh and through symbols (like the crucifix or cross) for the same reason we hang up wind chimes, to confirm for us that what we cannot see is there.

Cosmic wind chimes. Because we cannot see God, because we do not know God (or, rather, think that we cannot and do not), we hang them up, and by their presence amongst us we are reassured.

Thus, Jesus makes a sound and says to us, It is not I, but my Father Who speaks. Likewise, the wind blows, but the chimes sound. And hearing the chime, we say, "Listen to the wind!"

A wind chime does not need a wind chime. Nor do the Great Teachers need one another, or even themselves. They can see the wind.

They say to us, You will do as I have done, and more. You too can see the wind.

AUTHORS' NOTE

The contents of this book are drawn entirely from journals both of us have kept over the years since the beginning of our reach for Truth. They consist of observations each of us has made along our travel of the spiritual path. Although none was originally written for publication, we share them here in the hope that they might offer encouragement, guidance, or comfort to others in their own passage home.

We recognize that many of the entries in this book contradict one another. They were written over time by two individuals undergoing a continuing process of total transformation, and they reflect that fact. Thus, each expresses the perspective of its writer at the time of its writing. Also, the entries are not presented here in the order of their writing, or in any other particular order. Our view is that the book probably is best read in that random manner, too; that is, simply permit it to open where it will, and read there.

Every item was written by one or the other of us. None was written jointly, and neither did we ever synthesize or otherwise combine any of our journal entries into one "homogenized" version Thus, these reports are thoroughly individual and personal. For those readers who wish to know who wrote which, we have provided a breakdown of authorship at the end of the book.

Finally, we observe that the use of the masculine gender generally, in pronouns for the proper name God and in terms like man in the sense of mankind, is a grammatical option imposed by English. Neither of us used alternative constructions like he/she in our journals, and so we saw no need to do so here; they are too complicated, and ought to be unnecessary among those who are leaving behind the foolishness of chauvinism of every variety.

We bless this book, and we bless you, its reader.

LOVING ONE ANOTHER

If life is a process of relationship, then human love is sacred, because it is the process of losing oneself in another through relationship. It is a form of surrender, this relating to another, and in surrender is found the state of bliss which we all so longingly wish for.

Surrender of oneself to God, to a teacher, or to <u>any</u> person, event, thing, place, or whatever, in love, is relationship and guarantees bliss, just as human love, so long as it is self-less and surrendering, guarantees bliss. There is no difference in quality, no matter to <u>whom</u> or <u>what</u> we choose to surrender. It is the <u>process</u> of relating that is love, that is surrender, that is bliss.

The opposite of this process is selfishness, exclusiveness, or any other form of cutting oneself off from the process of relating, and it promises agony, discomfort, disease, and unhappiness.

This lesson can be very useful to those or us who find ourselves alone or in unavoidable, unpleasant situations. If we will surrender and relate to <u>everything</u> about us in the condition of aloneness, to the very God in that situation, we will not only escape the accompanying unhappiness, sorrow and discomfort, but find bliss, <u>even</u> in what might have seemed originally to be a disaster!

I AM HERE

I am not here to <u>anything</u>. I am simply here.

It is a question of seeing through and past the goal oriented perspective so indelibly imprinted upon this culture (or, should I say, this species). Long ago, someone somewhere convinced me that if I wasn't doing something, I wasn't doing anything, and ever since I have been busy making ends. Of late I notice that the more alert I am to this condition, the better I am at disguising my goals in the garb of service, or teaching, or healing. "These are important ends," I reassure myself, "and therefore worthy of my pursuit." Like the man said, wolves in sheep's clothing.

God's Purpose is simply to Be. I Am Here, He says, and He says no more, for I Am Here says it All. What's enough for the Father is enough for the Son.

I AM MY FATHER'S SON

Not "the only begotten Son of God", but the Son begotten only of God.

Or, consider carefully whom you call Father, for as you do, so it is.

PRECISELY HERE, TOGETHER

When I look at you, you think I am seeing what you think you look like and what you think you are. And when you look at me, I think you are seeing what I think I look like and what I think I am.

But, of course, it is not so. In fact, when you look at me, you perceive what you think I am. That is, you perceive in me what you think I ought to be based upon what your accumulated knowledge and experience and so on determine a "me" ought to look like, and act like, and be. And my perception of you is similarly shaped, or I should say, misshaped. So, you are relating to someone that I am not, and I am relating to someone you are not. And we are both confused, disappointed, and eventually angered, when the other inevitably fails to act or react "appropriately".

Naturally, neither of us is aware that this is what is going on. And we don't seem to want to be made aware of it, either.

Is it any wonder that we so rarely communicate effectively? Indeed, the wonder is that we communicate at all!

Clearly, the only way out of this mess is for me to stop looking at you as I do and to start seeing you as you are, and you likewise. But how do we do that? God knows, but perhaps we begin precisely here, by making this observation, together.

GOD TALK

Two people, interacting, seemingly "creating" an intermingling reality is what I see daily within relationships, in fact what constitutes "reality" as I see it with my eyes and senses. My question is always "How do they co-exist?" How is it possible, if there is only one God, to have seemingly discrete entities with seemingly divergent perspectives of reality, interact as a unitive whole, while still maintaining their discrete realities? And the answer is, they don't! These two are actually two apparently manifest ideas of the one God. Thus, they work together in one "world" or "body", which is God. They appear to us as two "people", but actually "they" are really God talking to Himself - rather like our own minds do all the time! They don't co-exist, they are two "images" of the one God. So you and I, talking together, are God talking to Himself. And this applies to all relationships, to all interactions; nothing is excluded!

"IN THE KINGDOM OF HEAVEN THERE IS NO MARRIAGE"

The body rations its energy evenly, nourishing every part equally and without exception, and thus it functions perfectly. In the body of heaven, relationships must be equally nourished, balanced, just as in the body of the human being. When it is not so, dis-ease occurs, both in the body human and in the body of heaven. Ask then if relations with others are balanced, and evenly dispersed, for if one takes or receives too much, or too little, the body of heaven will not run smoothly either.

A PERFECT APPLE

Imagine, if you will, an apple. Say, sitting on a plate on a table. On one side of the apple is a large rotten spot. Soft, brown, and spreading. It is a perfect apple.

A perfect apple? But what about the rotten spot? Yes, what about the rotten spot. Our insistence that only a blemish-free apple is perfect is a value judgment we have made based solely upon what we think we want and need, or, more generally, upon who and what we think we are.

The fact is that a rotten (or rotting) apple is a perfect apple; or, if you prefer, a rotting apple is being an apple perfectly. Apples rot. And thank God they do, or we would all be over our heads in apples! The rotten spot is a perfect rotten spot. If it were imperfect, it would not be rotting properly; or it wouldn't be on the apple where it belongs.

The world is perfect. That doesn't necessarily mean nice, any more than that the foregoing means we should pick rotten apples from the barrel to eat. But what it does mean is that whatever is happening is doing so perfectly, or precisely according to its nature at the moment of its occurring.

Seek Love, and know Perfection.
Seek perfection, and achieve arrogance.

NOT OURS, BUT HIS

This relationship we share, whoever you and I might be and whatever we may think is the nature of our relationship, is not mine and is not yours. It is not <u>our</u> relationship. It is God's. This relationship, this marriage between us, belongs to God; and it is designed and intended to serve only God's purposes.

God's purpose for this relationship is our spiritual growth or reawakening. And no other! Our function, and our only legitimate function, is to serve the relationship. Not ourselves, not each other, but the relationship. Only in doing so can we serve God, and again, only because the relationship is God's and not ours. Thus, we can serve God only indirectly, by serving what is God's, not directly. God does not need our service. The instant we forget that, we err.

Further, this relationship we share is not intended to fill or, for that matter, even address our desires or expectations. It will, however, serve our one only true need. We cannot effect the fulfillment of that need. Only God can do that. All we can do is permit the fulfillment of that need by not endlessly struggling against it. And we do that only by permitting the relationship to be and to perform its intended sacred purpose.

Consider it this way. Our relationship is like the soil in which we grow. God is the gardener. All of the intiative is God's. All of the planning, planting, and tending is performed by God. All of the seeds and all of the harvest belong to God. The very most that we can do is honor the gardener by honoring the garden.

WE ARE FREE

The path of love is a yoga or way of undoing. There are no particular practices or postures, no techniques to follow or do. The means is forgiveness, not of others but of ourselves.

The message of forgiveness is this: My perceived guilt is meaningless because my perceived crime was meaningless. Whatever I think I did occurred in a nonexistent place in an unreal time among nonexistent people. Thus, there is no point in trying to undo what I think I did, for doing so will only create more confusion for myself. Rather, I must seek to see what is as it is and not as I believe it to be, or as I fear it to be, or, in a word, as I now perceive it to be.

Curiously, this seems to have something to do with karma. Karma is in effect an agreement among us (you and me and all the rest of us) to reward or punish (as appropriate) ourselves for our perceived actions in this perceived world. That is, let's say, after you and I die this time around, we meet "up there" and after having inventoried and analysed this our most recent but now past life, we agree we have more to learn or unlearn and decide to "come back" (to reincarnate); further, and obviously I am grossly oversimplifying here, we agree to perform certain actions on or to each other which we have decided are appropriate or necessary to effect what we feel we want to accomplish, or are appropriate or necessary to accomplish what we believe we need. Thus, our experiences in our "next" life (the one which was the subject of this "conference" between you and me) truly are predetermined; not by some distant fate or impersonal destiny, but quite literally by you and me, and precisely because they are appropriate and necessary. Karma. From this perspective, of course, the doctrine of karma makes a lot of sense, particularly because it teaches so nicely the related ideas that choices have consequences and that all life is relationship. But - - and this is an important but - - the doctrine of karma depends upon our acknowledgment that this perceived world is real, and that likewise all the actions which occur here are similarly real. Once we recognize that none of it is real, at least not as we perceive it to be (and that distinction is crucial; indeed, it is the crux or the cross on which it all hangs!), we realize that the doctrine of karma in effect depends upon, or in effect is, the analysis of meaningless data and therefore must ultimately be meaningless itself.

Once again, then, the process of forgiveness says to us that so long as we choose to live in the world we now perceive, or so long as we choose to reinforce those perceptions by acting as if they were real, then we must and will live with the consequences of that choice, which the doctrine of karma defines very nicely. But whenever we are ready, we can choose to see it as it is, and then we will know that we are free, that we have always been free, and that we will always be free.

Whatever the question, God answers, Yes!
It's the only Word He Knows.
So, be careful what you ask.

I DID IT

You (whoever you may be who are the current target of my self-pity) did nothing to me. I did it (whatever it may be that is the current focus of my self-righteous resentment) to myself. And I did so by presuming that it (anything) could be done to me; that is, by considering myself to be weak, fragile, and vulnerable. And then blaming you both for that fact (which is and always was a figment of my imagination) and for having taken advantage of it (which you could not do as it is not really there to be taken advantage or anything else of).

So, what seems to have happened is this: I chose to perceive myself as I am not and to feel accordingly rotten, and then to project the whole thing onto you, and to blame you for it.

Thus, forgiveness (which is the only viable way out of this mess) has nothing to do with you, precisely because you have not done anything. Of course, I assume it has to do with you just as long as I continue to assume the problem is yours. But in fact forgiveness has to do with me, for forgiveness resides in my undoing the first error by seeing myself as I am in Truth. So-called inner work. The rest, like the Man said, will follow.

I AM WHAT

I am what God would have me be.
I am what God would be as me.
So, be it.

CONSIDERING LONELINESS

Loneliness seems real to those who are alienated. But if we truly love God and therefore His creatures, loneliness is non-existent.

Much as it may seem the contrary, loneliness is not dispelled by having many friends. If we are alienated from life, the most friends can do is put off or disguise our sense of loneliness. They can provide a superb distraction from our state of mind. But if our alienation prohibits our being intimate with them, then however much we surround ourselves with noise, people and activity, we remain lonely. Only God, through our love for Him, can remove our alienation and restore our ability to be intimate ... with friends and with strangers.

If you have one good friend, you don't need many. On the other hand, one good friend interferes with relationships with other friends. This applies as well to God, and in both directions.

Loneliness opens the heart, and makes us receptive to inner energies. It is good, in concentrated doses, from time to time.

It is essential if we wish to know God. The reason it works so well in this regard is that when the comfort of companionship and the "known" is gone, and we turn to God to alleviate the discomfort; and He comes in, because He has finally been invited!

We _must_ deal with real loneliness before death, precisely because it is the fear of loneliness that makes death so scary.

We are lonely because we _feel_ separated, which is only because of the apparent isolation of the body. That is why distance between two lovers seems to increase their loneliness. The physical separation underlines the seeming boundaries of the body which are more easily forgotten when we are in close proximity to each other. In a way, physical closeness seems to rub against the boundaries, diminishing them.

Loneliness is the sensation felt by one body as a result of the addiction to the presence of other bodies. That is all it is.

HERE'S THINKING OF YOU, KID

What we call the body and what we call the mind are two sides of the same coin. The mind is our thoughts (at every level - - that is, it is the content), and the body (and "its life") is the physical manifestation of our thoughts (at every level) or of the content. The body is the dramatization, to borrow a word, of the mind. Thus, our every action (or, more accurately, our life) is our thoughts manifested, or dramatized, or, if you like, the inner content "outer-ed". And every thought (at whatever level) "outers", or is manifested; has to be, for the one is the other.

To be sure, it seems that actions or events occur "spread out" over time while thoughts seem instantaneous, and so we see the two as being more in a cause-and-effect relationship. But that they seem so is simply a function (and perhaps the purpose) of time. In Truth, they "occur" simultaneously, because, again, the one is the other. So, thoughts do not cause actions, or events. Thoughts <u>are</u> actions or events (or, again, our life). The one is the thing seen from the inside, the other is the thing seen from the outside. So, we might say, my life (which is, of course, this world as perceived by me) is the mind seen from the so-called outside; and my thoughts (at every level) are the mind seen from the so-called inside.

Once again, like the man said: To change the outer, change the inner.

BORN TO THEM A MAN THOUGHT

Take away your name and <u>all</u> the thoughts, memories, expectations, attributes, experiences, characteristics, relationships, and so on that are in any sense associated with your name - - that is, utterly strip yourself of the identity provided by your name - - and what is left?

Consider this. When Stefan's parents chose to have a child, they thought to have a thought. They called that thought a child, and they named that child Stefan. They then set about shaping that thought (or that projected thought or thought form) into a configuration which pleased them based upon all their own programming (or shaping) received in turn from their parents. They taught what they called Stefan to speak as they did, to eat and dress as they did, to believe as they did, to look and act as they did; in every way they could think of to be as they were. We might say that they invested (from the Latin <u>investire</u>, to clothe in) the thought called "Stefan" with or of themselves, they clothed it in the stuff of them, so that it would be like them and continue after them (when the thought forms which their parents manifested, ceased; or, as we say, when they died).

Somehow, somewhere, I (whatever precisely that is) accepted identity with or as that thought (that is, I saw myself as being the same as that thought, so that I might say "I am Stefan", or, "Stefan and I are one"). When, at its birth, the thought's thinkers said to their new-born thought, "You are Stefan", for some reason I believed they were speaking to me, and I have acted accordingly **ever** since.

The question is, is that what I am now undoing? Am I unraveling my initial acceptance of that identity? And, if so, what will be left when I am done. How will I know when it's over? Who will be there to know?

THE SENSE OF GOD

The sense of being one with God, as opposed to one outside of God, and therefore separated, cannot truly be put in words. It is something which either we know or we see or we don't. It comes only when it comes.

In its initial revelation, it is awesome, and at the same time, so terribly obvious. But essential to experiencing this "sense" is the feeling of selflessness. The two concepts, 1) that I am a separate entity, or a separate identity, and, 2) the sense of being one with God, are mutually exclusive, or inimical to one another. They cannot abide together.

There is at the moment of understanding a temporary cessation of separateness. It is rather like viewing the world from God's eyes, for a moment. God doesn't come into "me", because "me" is not "a me" at the time of unity. Instead, "me" dissipates, evaporates, for an instant. Understand that if God is <u>all</u> there is, I cannot be one with Him at all, and as God <u>is</u> all there is, <u>all</u> aspects of the universe are God, including me, and you, and them, so when feeling one with God, <u>I</u> am not feeling anything, because <u>I</u> cannot be <u>both</u> me and God, if God is all there is. There cannot be separation, or division, of an indivisible one, which is what God is. Thus, there cannot be a separate "I" when "I" am one with God. There can only be a separate "I" when I feel apart from God, separated out, alienated from the whole, alone and isolated.

This sense of a separate I is a choice we make, and most of us do just that, but it is not inevitable. It is our option to seek out the truth and to fully realize who and what we are. We cannot realize our continuity with a indivisible one and leave <u>anything</u> out. Likewise, if we wish to be separate, then others have to be also. In fact, it is when an ego-centric, or separated individual, who has not surrendered his ego to the concept of unity, perceives or senses his oneness with God, and returns to his original separated state without proper understanding of what is occurring, that mental imbalance can result. Why he or she was permitted a glimpse into this great truth when he or she wasn't prepared is a question I cannot answer. Perhaps it is the forbidden fruit of the tree of life, eaten before it was time. Disobedience and temper tantrums at an early age; some of us do that!

In any event, surrender to this unity or at least understanding and willingness to surrender, is essential if we are to ever fully experience and incorporate this sense of oneness with God into our life. Without surrender, we only accumulate ideas of ideas, concepts of "hidden" knowledge, but not the "knowledge" itself. Because this sense of unity is not conveyed by the mind, but by the heart, by the whole being to the whole being. It can be intimated or suggested by the mind to another mind, but only the "heart" can "know" it, can hold it, can "see" it. This "seeing" of course is an inner knowing, characterized by the "eureka" of moments of enlightenment.

When this knowing really sinks in, it is scary. For we realize suddenly in all its entirety the awesome responsibility we have to ourself. On the other hand, we realize it doesn't matter, because if <u>all</u> is God and God is good, then <u>whatever</u> is done is God and therefore good. Thus, the idea of responsibility vanishes. For how can anyone be responsible if there are no "others" to be responsible to in the first place?

NOT EVEN A PENNY

Jesus said, "He who sins is a slave to sin." Just so, we who think, are slaves to our thoughts. We cannot be free of them, of where they lead us and of how they bog us down, except by not thinking them. The only way out from under them is to stop thinking them.

We cannot control our thoughts, for so long as we think, whatever we think, it is our thoughts which control us. Indeed, it is our thoughts which <u>are</u> us. Descartes has been widely applauded for his observation, "I think, therefore I am"; applauded by the thoughts of other thinkers, that is, for our thinking is their very life. The fact is, when I think, I am not. Thinking does not establish being; thinking distracts from being.

Think about it. It is impossible to think in the present. Every thought we think is from the past, every concept or mental image is inherited or adopted, at the very earliest a moment ago. We may project it into the future or onto what we think is the present, but it's always yesterday's data. Thus, instead of experiencing what is happening now, we are thinking about it, measuring it, comparing it, judging it, all in yesterday's terms. Or indexing it into the museum of our mind, for retrieval later. Like spending an entire vacation taking photographs to look at later. Little wonder so many of us die asking ourselves, "Where did my life go?" We missed it. We weren't there. We were either getting ready for it or looking back on it. We spent the whole time thinking about it.

KNOWLEDGE IS

In Love, I do not need to know anything until I need to know it, and knowledge is provided when it is appropriate or necessary. But not as a thing which I have, like a possession, as I think of knowledge now, but rather as an attribute or characteristic of what I am at this instant (that is, "One who knows whatever needs to be known whenever").

Thus, it is not that in Love one "knows everything" like some giant walking/talking computer data bank. After all, what would one want all that information _for_? Rather, it is that one's being or self is or includes the information (and everything else) necessary and appropriate to whatever situation or happening is unfolding or arising at any and every moment.

In the world, knowledge is power and to be craved and guarded jealously. That is as it is in the world, which knows and understands nothing. To those who know Love, knowledge is simply another word for God, infinitely here and everywhere all the time, appearing variously but always appropriately.

Consider it this way: Knowledge as we understand it consists in knowing others. That is, knowledge is what is required to live successfully in this world, or to function effectively separatively. Wisdom, we might say, is knowing ourself. Wisdom, then, represents the first step away from knowledge in the direction of Love, from the outer toward the inner. Here, although we still live in this world, our focus or primary attention is shifted from the the many to the one. Finally, intelligence, or enlightenment, is knowing nothing, or rather no thing. Every instant is complete and completely every instant. Whatever is required exists, and everything that exists is required. The One is whole, and there is no other, not even a sense of "no other".

This is Love, and it is already.

THOUGHTS ABOUT GOD

God requires everything of us! We can belong to no one else if we wish to belong to Him. This is particularly hard because it means entering a sense of rootlessness as we drop all our past, all our associations, all our values, indeed, all our roots! Of course, all the while, the seeker has the greatest of roots in the Godhead, But, it takes time to find those. It is a lonely process, even terrifying sometimes. Like being on the very edge of madness, the insecurity and uncertainty it imposes. Sometimes it seems to be too much. But, we survive!

The reason to isolate ourselves occasionally, or often, as the case may warrant, is this: Isolating us may be the only way God can get our attention. When other human beings are present, they are a source of distraction and often demand our attention. But alone, in retreat, there is no one to turn to or to occupy us; there is finally silence and God can be heard. Sometimes retreats, or periods of isolation, may be very long!

When God says "you will have no other Gods but Me" He means that to apply to everything. We must depend on Him totally, completely, and on no one and nothing else but Him. This is essential to see God. When we do this fully and always, everything disappears; needs, homes, things, others, and finally, but not least of all, thoughts! (which are the source of all the rest). This is the transcendent process. By having only God, there _is_ only God.

MORE THOUGHTS ABOUT GOD

The great fear of losing one's identity associated with surrender to God is nonesense. We confuse identity with separateness. In surrender to God, we do lose our separateness, but we do not lose our sense of identity, of being.

Separateness is the sense of being isolated, different from others, or unique. Many of us erroneously consider this to be our individuality or identity. In truth, identity is the state of beingness, the consciousness of being alive, the certain knowledge that I am. This sensation is God expressing and feeling Himself, and our recognition of it awakens us to our true identity.

What I call the spark of God in man is really the small aperture of memory I have of who I am. Please note that in the use of "I", it is always capitalized. Not so with you, me, he and it. Could there be a clue here?

IT IS SUNLIGHT

Observe that it is sunlight which gives to each planet its "life" but that the light is not itself of the planet. Indeed, the light is not really even in the planet. It is simply there, unconditionally passing through, one might say, and it is that fact, the light's presence, which provides, or should we say permits, the condition we call life. (I wonder what the light calls this condition?) Thus, the earth is alive because of the light from the sun which the earth reflects. Notice too that if we remove the planet the light "disappears". That is, pitch black darkness returns to the spot in space formerly occupied by the planet. Of course, in truth the light has not gone anywhere, not having actually "been" there in the first instance. Rather, it appeared there because of the presence of the planet to reflect it.

So, for the existence of the light we depend upon the sun. However, to be aware of the light, or for the light to be visible, we depend upon the existence of the planet, something to reflect the light; and we call that reflection life. Thus, although the light can exist well enough on its own, it cannot be seen or known to exist (perhaps even to itself) without something like a planet to reflect it.

God, we are told, created us in His own Image. Thus, we are a reflection of God. Or, God is reflected in or by us. It is the reflection of that light, His Light, which makes our life possible; indeed, which is our life. Remove God and we are dead, even non-existent. Remove us and God does not cease to exist, but He does cease to be known, perhaps even to be knowable, maybe even to Himself. Without us to reflect His Light, it would simply be, in pitch black darkness.

If God is life to us, maybe we can say that we are Self-

Consciousness to Him. Without Him, we are not; without us, He doesn't know He is.

My God, He needs me!

LIKE FATHER, LIKE SON

When Jesus says to us, "Call no man your father on earth, for you have one Father, who is in heaven," we all applaud (Isn't it wonderful how we admire him!) and then carry on as if he had said nothing of the kind.

> Recognize the distractions.
> Minimize the distractions.
> Eliminate the distractions.
> So help me, God.

INFINITY IS INFINITE

All of God's characteristics must be infinite because Infinity, which is one of His characteristics, is itself obviously infinite and thus must pervade everything else about Him. Thus, God's Love, God's Wisdom, God's Vision, and so on, must all be Infinite, each sharing the common trait, Infinity, which, once again, being infinite is everywhere and into everything all the time or, more accurately, timelessly. And, if each of His characteristics is infinite, then they must likewise infinitely pervade each other, so that, for example, His Love is inifitely Wise, His Wisdom infinitely Loving, and so on.

Similarly, we too must be Infinite and in our every respect, just as He is. As our Creator, God could not have given us what He Himself did not have (that is, finite-ness) but only what He did have. And whatever He chose to give us, it had also to be infinite, for, as we have seen, everything He has, or is, is infinite. In this regard, imagine a man working with clay who has a tube strapped to his arm through which a constant flow of green paint splashes out over his hands. Everything he makes, whatever its intended or apparent shape, form, or purpose, will be infused and colored by green paint. Within and without, it will all be green. Likewise, everything God creates, everything He even considers, is filled with and shares His Infinity.

Thus, we are Infinite, and if we think that we are not, as most of us do, then that misconception will itself be infinite and will infinitely pervade or color our every other thought, and our lives will indeed seem, as indeed they do, infinitely finite! The only way out of this mess is to change our sense of ourselves, to start perceiving ourselves as infinite. That perception, being itself infinite, will invade our every other perception, and soon enough we will begin to recognize its color in every aspect of our lives. There will be green all over! Where we had perceived limits and boundaries, walls and barriers, we will now see endless horizons, empty, free space.

We will have reclaimed for Infinity its proper home, ourselves. To be sure, it is not as easy as it sounds, but it is that simple.

NOTHING TO FEAR

If God is Infinite and therefore wholly everywhere always, there can be nowhere, no when, and no thing that He is not. Therefore, it cannot be other than that God is all there is. Thus, whatever I see or in any other way experience is God; there is nothing else it can be. And whatever is seeing or in any other way experiencing is God. Even seeing or experiencing is God. Everything is God and nothing is not God.

Thus baptized, the Universe is safe. There are no enemies.

With nothing to fear, I rest my defenses.

Free at last.

Thank God.

THINKING ABOUT THOUGHT

Mentality, or mental work, cannot fully remove the fear of disease or disease itself. The only reason that there is disease and the fear of disease is because we believe in a system of thought that requires "good and bad" concepts (disease and health, for example). As this belief system, which is the basis of our thought process, is held by the collective unconscious (by all thought producing entities on earth), and as long as we buy into that mode of thought, which we do on a moment to moment basis - <u>all</u> our thoughts depend on opposites - then we, as a part of that collective unconscious are inevitably subject to its rules and regulations.

Simple substitution of positive thought for negative thought, while this helps to open the door to healing, or better, to God, is not sufficient for full and final healing. Releasing the mind to God's care is the ultimate requirement for success in healing. We must stop everything, pray, and give it to God. Not just once, but over and over again, until this state of surrender erases and supercedes all other thoughts or reactions. Then, true healing begins. Do not mistake this point! Thought as we know it, as human thought, is human, not celestial. Surrender and worship in God's light and love express true intelligence and that comes only with the hushing of thought, the emptying of the vessel before filling it with God's spirit.

Of course, one <u>can</u> use affirmative thought to counteract negative thought, and this will work, but only for a while, and only while practised. That is, with human thought alone, one can stop or slow the manifestations of any particular disease, but not "cure" it. Until we release the concept of "good as opposed to bad" (wellness as opposed to disease), we will always have "bad" to contend with. This is simply the nature of human thought, which is dual. But by turning to God, by, in effect, letting God think for us, we can become perfect as <u>God</u> sees perfection, not as <u>we</u> see it. Besides, we don't understand what perfect is. After all, thinking as we do now we are too ignorant and limited in vision to understand what perfect is. Indeed, often what turns out to be best for us seems "bad" at the outset, and, if we had our own way then, if we were able to "heal" ourselves out of what was unfolding, we would miss the ultimate "perfect" resolution. The fact is, we don't know what is best for us.

DIFFERENT THOUGHTS

There are two kinds of thought. One, which is based on opposites, the other, on wholeness. "Good and bad" are of the former, quieting of the mind is of the latter. Healing of a lasting effect occurs from the latter; short term healing, if at all, from the former. So, when we heal ourselves through affirmation, through so-called positive thinking, only to find later that some other illness has overtaken us, we might ask ourselves whether we have surrendered and are letting God "think" for us, or whether we are still thinking for ourselves.

STOPPING THOUGHT

It is not that we must work at stopping thought. Rather it is self-consciousness that must cease. Thought will cease with the cessation of self-consciousness.

It is self-consciousness (this small self) which creates tension, division, and separation, and which therefore blocks the flow, in and out, of the universal energy. Give it up, this self-consciousness, and the flow begins again.

TRANSCENDENCE OF THOUGHT

A "change" of thought patterns is not what is at work in healing, but a "transformation", and thereby "transcendence", of our minds. The importance of looking toward wholeness and love cannot be overstressed. When we emphasize the power of mentality, the exclusive use of our human thoughts, and leave out the "feeling" of wholeness and love, we end up with incomplete results. Only to "change" the mind implies the potential for changing back again. We find ourselves dealing with two things again, the former state, and the "changed " state, which involves duality, and thus "un-wholeness", fragmentation, a state that is not eternal, but changing. Transformation of thought, or ultimately transcendence, eliminates that possibility because in transcendence of thought, we no longer "think" dually, and therefore can "think eternally", in a "whole" manner. (Of course, transcendence of thought means we no longer "think", but we are still aware, and thus I have used "think" in a very loose sense here.)

Another way of saying this is, when we have only changed our mind from bad thoughts to good thoughts, negative concepts to positive concepts, we have merely substituted one set of thoughts or preferences for another, and we know it. We know we are dealing with limited and opposite concepts, and we therefore know we are limited and the results will be limited. We need instead a sense of expansion, wholeness, "greaterness", which comes only through transcendence. The initial commitment to transformation of thoughts is what facilitates that transcendence. Of course, this cannot be achieved otherwise than through surrender or loss of our separate small mind or "self" in exchange for God or Self. Thus, transformation, and thereby transcendence, is not a question of changing ourselves but of giving up ourselves.

THOU SHALT HAVE NO GODS

Let's face it, sooner or later we are going to have to release and give up even God. Just like everything else in our brains, God is no more than a symbol for the Real, for Love, a symbol created by us for use in the world. And if to know the Truth that we are, we must die to the lie that we perceive ourselves to be, then clearly all of the stuff of that lie, all of the thoughts, memories, names, devices, images, expectations, and so on, which go into it, however lofty and sacred, have to go as well.

After all, at the very least, our continuing to perceive God as we do grants continued life to the distortion that there is a God and a we, which, dear friends, there simply is not. Notwithstanding the fact that God as a symbol may stand for everything good and wonderful in the Universe, His existence (or Hers; it doesn't make any difference as ultimately both are equally absurd) in our mind as an other remains an obstacle in our way to the Truth (Which is that there are no others). That is, if God is all there Is, then our continued insistence that He is something and we are something else, is clearly wrong. If there is only One, then either He doesn't exist or we don't, or He and we are One and the same. Whatever the case, we have got to stop talking about Him, and about each other and everything else, as if there were two or more.

"Sooner or later we are going to have to" do this, we said at the outset. Thank God it doesn't have to be right now. After all we've given up already, I'm not sure I'm ready to give Him up, too. Or is it that I'm not ready to give me up? Is it perhaps not the continued existence of Him but the continued existence of me which is the obstacle in the way of there being only One. If, as we have said, He is the One, then we must be the other! And in a Universe of only One, it is the other which has to go.

WHEN I LOOK AT GOD

When I look at God, I see myself. And I place on God, or perceive in God, the same attributes, the same limitations, as I place on or perceive in myself. Thus, I see God as a separate entity (that is, separate from me, or "up there" somewhere) just as I see myself as separate from others, although by lip service I insist on the unity of all life. Similarly, I perceive God as working in time and space, and as limited by those boundaries precisely because I see myself so limited; so that I do not really expect any genuine "miracles" in my life, like turning stones into bread and the like, even though I insist by lip service that God is omnipotent. I even imagine God as having emotions and experiencing joy, anger, and remorse, as I do, even though by lip service I would insist that God is eternal love and peace and bliss. In sum, I suppose, I perceive God as some kind of immense me. Bigger, better, wiser, stronger, but still about the same. Of course, the perceived evidence of God in my life is exactly proportional to the nature of God as I perceive it. That is, I perceive His presence precisely as I see Him: limited.

On the other hand, when God looks at me, He sees Himself with all of His own attributes (the ones I pay lip service to, like omnipotence and so on). And presumabaly He sees me in every aspect of everything, or everywhere, for He sees me as being, again, like Him, or Infinite. Clearly, the question is, why don't I see myself the way He sees me. Why won't I take His Word for it?

FEAR OF CHANGE, OR THE EVIL ONE

Every action is God-action, <u>every</u> action, even seemingly evil action, for how are we to be judges of what is evil action? We cannot see the full forest; we see only one tree, not recognizing that it takes many trees to make up a forest.

What may seem evil to one, may be a blessing to another. For example, suppose a woman is on illicit drugs, a woman catapulting herself nowhere in desparation, wasting her energy. She is arrested for drug abuse and possession, and put in jail; there, she contacts a deadly disease from the use of dirty needles. From there, she is transfered to a prison hospital, where perhaps for the first time in her life, she is exposed to a genuinely loving person, perhaps in the form of her nurse, who introduces her to some spiritual text, and her life changes. She becomes a new woman. Which part of this story is evil?

It is the change, is it not, that <u>seems</u> evil? The results, if we will move freely with the change, are almost always, are always, good, better changed. It is our resistance to change that obstructs, and, through that resistance, creates what we perceive as evil in the first place.

So, it follows then that all steps "along the way" are good, right and perfect. It is only when we let ourselves stagnate, when we rest at a step too long that the "evil one", resistance to change, reigns. Fear of change stops change, stops progress, prevents movement, creates mires. <u>There</u> is evil, which is, again, merely fear, fear of change.

What is lack of faith, loss of faith, or any variation of that, after all, but again, simply, fear of change? The seeker who flows with God, who surrenders all to God, is merely expressing faith, the faith that change (for as long as we live, there must be change; even a breath, in and out, is change) will not harm him, and faith that change is good, is God. In fact, then, faith in God is faith in change, that all change is good, which is God.

Do not resist, for resistance is evil. How clear it is! The resistance (which can only be to change, for what else is there to resist?) is the creation of evil, pure and simple. It is not "out there'; it is "in here". Consider any form of evil; is it not at base resistance to change? War, famine, hatred, jealousy, greed, etc., they all come about through resistance to change. In a war between two individuals or two nations, hatred or animosity is born from the insistence that "he, or they, don't believe the way I do, or he, or they are forcing me to change my beliefs, to consider another point of view; therefore, I hate him, or them, because they won't play the game by my rules, and I certainly don't want to change to his." Greed comes from the fear of losing what I already have, of changing from a have to a have not, on a small or large scale, it all amounts to the same motivation, to keep what I have at all costs, and to resist any change to a different state or situation. Even death seems "evil" because of our enormous resistance to change, to the transformation of our bodies to other "states", and our consciousness to different modes of consciousness, and thus we will endure almost any cost to avoid the inevitable and natural transformation of bodies, not realizing that we, as God, are actually changeless, and thus do not need to resist anything.

However, if one can bring oneself to see that change in the physical world is of God and through God, not just some but <u>all</u> change, then whatever occurs, in whatever disguise, whether it seems pleasant or unpleasant, <u>becomes</u> God; change becomes simply God being God, and there is no evil anymore. If the change is good (Godly), it is good, pure and simple, which is God, and thus miraculously perfect.

STOPPING FEAR

How to stop fear? "Stop doing that!"

We are actually simply scaring ourselves with self-generated imagined terror. And the way to stop is to tell ourselves to "Stop doing that!". If we do this over and over again, it will stop the process.

Easy, isn't it? And it works!

THE PATH OF THE WARRIOR

Courage must be created, developed in the aspiring lover of God. Without courage, nothing can be accomplished.

Women seem to be at a particular disadvantage here. In their youth, courage is not developed in them, but instead it is something often deprecated, considered to be too masculine and not appropriate or "lady like". Even Jesus is said to have remarked about Mary Magdelene "I shall make her a man." Could he have been referring to this very phenomenon?

The way to God is not for the weak or the timid. It is the path of the warrior, and the qualities of a warrior, if we don't already have them, must be adopted, nourished and cultivated. We must drop all our affectations and overcome the propensity to lean on others for strength; and we must develop inner confidence and certainty, and permit the growth of self-esteem. All of this can only be accomplished through determined inner work and hard discipline.

Courage, which is derived from the French word "coeur" for heart, the place we point to when we think of ourselves, the residence of God within us, is, after all, the foundation of God realization.

THE ILLUSION IS

The world is not an illusion. In fact, the illusion is that the world is the world and not God. So long as we perceive the two as separate, God on the one hand, the world on the other, so long as we perceive them as two!, we labor under a delusion, the delusion that they are two. <u>That</u> is the illusion.

One way to see this identity of the world and God is to let ourselves be the world totally, without any reservations. Absolutely to immerse ourselves in the world, free of every judgment about it and any consideration of anything greater or better than it. That is, free of a sense of God beyond the world. Then we can experience the awareness that the world is all there is, and that that all includes, or is too, God. The illusion of a separation between the two, between God and the world, vanishes. We see that the world and God are One and the same: knowing the world, we know God; being the world, we are God.

This way is what I believe the Hindu tradition means by tantra yoga, and it is very risky. We in the West are particularly disinclined towards it because we insist on seeing spirituality as a means to something else, something "better", and thus we are most reluctant to permit our participation in the world, even for "spiritual" reasons, to be whole, free, unassuming and unreserved. We distrust the world, and so we cannot believe that it is God. More than anything, we want out of the world, not deeper in. But in fact we are all struggling with it (the world, our lives, ourselves) so desperately and constantly that we do not know what it means, or what it feels like, really to be in the world. We think we do, but we have never truly tried it, except perhaps in infancy, when it was all one to us anyway.

THE WORLD IS

In the spiritual context or sense of the word, "the world" is, or equals, or is the same as, perceiving and experiencing separatively. Separative means there is you, and there is me, and there is everything else. It is, of course, all God, but it is not perceived so to the observer, because the observer (you and me) perceives himself as other than.

Liberation, which is the unspeakable opposite of the world, is, or equals, or is the same as, seeing and knowing One. There is God, and God is all there is, and all that is is God. It is not only a fact, as indeed it always was, but now it is known to be true; not believed, but known.

At any given moment, we are doing one or the other totally and only, for we cannot simultaneously serve two masters, even sort of. Either I perceive you or I see Me.

Whether I choose to perceive separatively or not does not change God or the world or anything else. Nothing can do that. But if I change the way I see, or the eyes I see by, then everything will look changed to me, including myself. So, the Teachers tell us, in effect, don't wash the dirt; see it clean.

OUT OF SHAPE

There are those in physics today who believe (as I understand it) that what you and I consider to be material reality is in fact nothing more than a curvature in or a bending of the so-called space-time continuum. That is, the universe is in effect bent, and it is that bend which creates the appearance of "substance".

Consider it this way. By being bent, or by bending itself, the universe is able to look back on itself, to reflect upon itself. The bending creates an apparent surface against or on which the light, let°s say, of the universe can reflect or be reflected, creating the appearance or illusion of something being there, like the moon's reflection in a puddle. It isn't really there, but it surely seems to be there. And it is that something, that reflection, which we are.

Remove the puddle, and the reflection disappears. Not the moon, you understand, but the reflection. Similarly, make straight the Universe, and we disappear. Again, not the Universe, which some might prefer to call God, but the reflection or the image.

Now, the question is, is it that the universe is bent, or is it that our perception of it is bent? In other words, are we looking crooked at the thing, and wondering why it apears crooked to us. If so, the answer is not to straighten out the thing, but ourselves. Turn ourselves right side up, and presumably we will stop seeing it upside down!

WHEN WATER FALLS

Consider this. When water descends from a cloud, it falls as snow on the mountaintop and as rain in the valley.

When it falls as rain in the valley, it is not snow acting as rain; and when it falls as snow on the mountaintop, it is not rain acting as snow. Rather, it is in both instances water relating absolutely and appropriately to the environment or nature of the moment. It is always water being water. Not acting, but being.

To be sure, from the perspective of the observers at the scene, the water seems in each instance to be very different. To the one, it is soft and warm, nourishment for the grass and cleansing to the body. To the other, it is crystal and cold, cozy from the inside, invigorating on the outside, and stupendous on the slopes. To the water, it is water. Always only water.

Thus we are taught, be who you are where you are. Do not carry with you the who you were where you were; indeed do not even recall it, for then you are acting. Then, you are snow from the mountaintop acting as rain in the valley. Then, as snow in the valley you will judge the valley, comparing it to your place at the soaring peaks above, and likely find it wanting, when all along it is you who are amiss. Or, as rain on the mountaintop acting as snow, you will shiver at the bitter temperatures and long for your valley home.

Now, be who you are where you are does not mean, whining, "Must I come down to their level?" Water does not become rocks or trees or grizzly bears as it falls from the cloud. Water becomes what is appropriate to water in the conditions of the moment. And, come to think of it, it is never appropriate to water to compare itself, favorably or unfavorably, to rocks or trees or grizzly bears. For, in the final analysis, water <u>does</u> become rocks and trees and grizzly bears, appropriately when it is appropriate.

So, the Teacher might have said, where there is water, there am I; but look closely, and quietly, lest you fail to recognize me. Or, if you prefer, where there is life, there am I. But, again, don't expect me to seem as I seemed to you somewhere else, for here I am another. Perhaps you.

From God's perspective, I do not exist. After all, if I did, who would I be?

From God°s perspective, there is only He, and no other. Therefore, no me.

Who, then, am I? It seems there are only two possible choices. Either (1) I too am He (or, if you prefer, He is I), or (2) I am not.

Both, of course, are True.

WHO GENERATES NEEDS?

All our "needs" are generated by the body. They are "bodily needs." When I realize that I am not limited to the body, I see that there is something <u>behind</u> or <u>transcendent</u> to the body, <u>behind</u> all of it, behind even the universe. Then, the needs of the body become secondary, irrelevant.

There is the real me (which <u>always</u> includes you and all others), (the I Am), supporting or informing or infusing all of it, including my body and all other bodies. I (which <u>always</u> includes ...) have (as I Am) narrowed the vision down to the body only, excluding everything else as "not me", when in fact it is <u>all</u> me, only I (which <u>always</u> includes...), (the I Am), forgot! Or was educated out of the knowledge, conditioned away from this awareness, because, unfortunately and surprisingly, it seems that once lost our initial tendency is not to refind ourselves but to increase our numbers, even at the cost of causing others to lose their way too.

But, having seen all this, I can begin to refocus my attention and energy away from the body and its needs which I know are not my own, and back to rediscovering and reclaiming who I am.

THE ZOO FENCE

It's a body. Why not simply let it be one? Instead of fussing over it so much, worrying about its wealth, health, diet, looks, wardrobe, family, living accomodations, longevity, destiny, and God knows what else, just relax and observe it. See it live, look at what it does, listen to what it says. Like at a zoo, lean on the fence, and watch.

Who knows, you could learn something. At the very least, you might find it amusing.

LISTEN TO ME

There is a terrible tendency among us human beings to take ourselves and our activities altogether too seriously. While I have not been able precisely to identify the exact reason for this phenomenon, I suspect it has something to do with the fact that we can hear ourselves talk.

A BEING HUMAN

Not a human being, but a being human.

Think about it. A human being doesn't make sense. I mean, a human being what? A human isn't being anything, except perhaps human, but that's simply circular reasoning and means nothing.

But a being human. That is something else altogether. Here, the focus is not on what the human is being, but on what is being human. That is, not a human being anything, but a something being human. And what is that something? What, or who, is it that is being human? That is being me? That is being you?

Thus, the question becomes, is there something that is being us? And if so, what is it? Where is it? Can you see it in the mirror? Look carefully, behind the eyes, deep within. What's in there? Listen carefully. Can you hear it, in the silence, breathing, creating, being. Without letting on, observe yourself carefully, covertly. Like a cat beside a mouse hole, sit, wait, watch, as long as it takes. There's something in there alright, something being human, and if you wait patiently enough, quietly enough, sooner or later it will show itself.

THERE IS NO I

There is no "I" that lives "my life". There is only the process called "my life" which is happening, or being. However, it is not happening "to me". Rather, one might say I am it, or it is me experienced or observed in that way. My life is the I AM or The Universe being me. Thus, my life is all there is, or all there is is my life. Your life is all there is, too. After all, from the perspective of your life, your life is "my life".

So, it's a matter of perspective. There is the I AM, also known as God, and that is all there is. But it perceives itself variously, or from various perspectives, which we think are we.

Of course, being infinite (or, all there is), God, or The Universe, is wholly in everything that there is (or that it is). Thus, everything being wholly God, everything is the same. Not similar, but the same. To be sure, it seems to us that "each thing" is different or separate from each other thing, but that is only because it is in the nature of "my life" to perceive that way. When my life ceases to perceive separatively, it ceases to be "my life". It isn't that I cease to exist, for I never did exist. Rather, it is that God ceases to perceive Himself as me, or, actually, as my life. Your life, which as we have seen is in fact also "my life", continues unabated; until, that is, God chooses to cease seeing Himself that way, too!

ILLUSION

The entire world, or manifest universe, is a dream, literally created by thought, or mind. The thought doesn't "cause" the world "out there," it *is* the world, in here. If this is true, and I am certain it is, then all thought is interconnected (because thought is not "material" but is "fluid" and malleable, not static or isolated), and all thoughts of all beings come from a common source. A proof of this is: One's thoughts can impinge on, and often change, another's thoughts. This can be accomplished simply by more powerful and directed thought being introduced, either verbally or telepathically, to an "other", thereby changing the thoughts of the "other". A very common and obvious example of this phenomenon is commercial advertising.

If this is so, and I know that it is because I have seen it occur, then that "other" cannot be an other in actuality. It must be an extension of, say, me, in thought, because otherwise how can prayer, which is nothing other than directed thought, or any other thought, have any affect whatsoever on an entity with which I am presumably *not* connected?

If this is so, then in prayer all sorts of miracles and changes can occur, because prayer is recourse to the "source" of all thought, with the belief (a thought in itself) that that source is "all powerful", more powerful than one which is limited and therefore less than all-encompassing (me, or any other entity).

If this is so, and, fortunately, it is, then the act of praying is actually creating, through "God" (again, the source of all thought ultimately), a different world, and if it so happens that the prayer concerns another being, then the life of that other being is directly and immediately affected.

In other words, in order for prayer to be effective, which it can be, there must be some sort of identity that is common to us both, the "pray-er" and the "prayer-ee". And if that is so, the only common ground that I can find, the only activity which seems to be shared in this event, is prayer itself, or thought.

If this is so, then it is proof that the world as composed of multiples of separate, definable entities is in fact simply a creation of thought, or thought is the substratum of these multiples. It is a dream (and therefore an illusion), because otherwise it could not possibly be so malleable and susceptible to change simply through the exercise of a "non-physical" activity such as thought (or prayer). And certainly, were this not true, a directed thought that I might have could not possibly have an effect on another entity.

Thus, there is in fact no separate identity, no others, no "beings" in actual fact, because if there were separate beings, then this function of thought could not prevail, it could not do what it in fact does. It could not change the world and events of others, as it does.

My thoughts, and these thoughts of others, are all "sub" thoughts of the source thought, which is God. It is only because of our link to the source of thought that we are in fact able to think at all, and that our thoughts are capable of changing the environment or of affecting anything. This is our "God-like attribute", our capacity to think, and to the extent that it is all inclusive and non-separative -- in other words, closer to what it is in actuality, and not obstructed by individualized concepts -- it will be more and more effective in altering the world, and affecting greater expanses of the universe. The interconnectedness of all beings through the exercise and the transformative power of thought is proof of the wholeness of the universe, or God being that universe, and the illusory concept of individual entities. Once again, this has to be true because we could not affect the mind of "another" if that mind were in fact "separate." Rather, we can only affect the mind of "another" because it is somehow a "part" of us, because we are common to each other, because there is no "separation."

However, in so far as one entity thinks or believes that he is separate and bodily limited, then the ability to change any aspect of that body or the world of that limited body will be likewise limited and therefore difficult, if not impossible. This is the other side of the coin, of course. This also may explain the failures in prayer and other thought-control efforts by even the greatest of masters to alter the situation of another being who insists on remaining separate and isolated, who isn't, as it were, playing the game by the same rules as the master. This also explains why a separately "inclined" entity cannot successfully alter his own or another's environment, no matter how hard he may try. There is fortunately a fail-safe mechanism in this truth!

Eventually, we are forced to ask: Who is it that is actually directing our prayer? Who is it that watches the picture change? Who is it that "knows" this fact right here and now? Who is it that saw and sees that the illusion is an illusion? Who sees all and knows all this? Certainly not "I" who am a jumble of accumulated thoughts, either chosen or unchosen, and who surely cannot see beyond its own nose! The answer to that question will answer all questions!

As an afterthought to the preceding observations, we might conclude that, if all beings are indeed one and all thought is therefore common, then we do well to consider carefully whom we associate with and live near. For example, in living amongst "saints", or any other "spiritually inclined beings", we will be changed simply by being in proximity to their higher thoughts.

This assumes, of course, that we are open to, and not resisting those thoughts! And, if we can't find saints, then surely we can at least find people whose thoughts are "higher", more integrated or "whole" than our own. Change will occur to us precisely because we are nothing but thought, and therefore we will be affected by the predominating thought patterns or content wherever and with whomever we happen to be. Being nothing other than a creation of thought, we must take shape and be expressed according to the prevailing thought that is "there", <u>at that time</u> (in space, in time). It is simply common sense!

MASTERS

One cannot judge whether a master, or any kind of teacher for that matter, is good or bad. Because the judge (we) has an incorrect, incomplete, defective or mechanical (learned and previously conditioned), and, therefore, not objective, mind doing the judging. Therefore, whole-heartedly to embrace the paradigm of any master or teacher is better than holding on to one's "own" paradigm (values), because at least change, growth, and hopefully, expanded vision will take place. Otherwise, we stagnate. That is why surrender to the teacher, or God, or Christ, or whoever's paradigm we choose to surrender to, is essential. Because if we don't abandon, growth, change, and greater understanding which in turn leads to enlightenment, cannot occur.

THAT IS THE QUESTION

Imagine if the character Hamlet were to ask his creator, William Shakespeare, "What am I?" Who would be speaking? I mean, Hamlet is not really a person. Any words that might come from his mouth will have to have been put there by Shakespeare himself.

And to whom would he be speaking? Presumably, Hamlet could speak to Shakespeare only in the context of a play in which Shakespeare, as the author, had inserted himself as a character, as a theatrical ploy. But it would not really be as if Hamlet and Shakespeare were actually conducting a conversation. Rather, the character Hamlet and the character Shakespeare would be having a conversation in a play in which both parts (indeed, all parts) were written by the author Shakespeare, the only one of the lot of them who is real. The one who is the creator of it all, you might say.

What has this got to do with us? To be or not to be.

A FRIENDLY UNIVERSE

Whatever faces you, if God made it, it's harmless.

If God didn't make it, it doesn't exist, and so is equally harmless.

So what's there to be afraid of?

I'LL BUY THAT

Our reach for things in our search for happiness is absurd. Why do we insist they will bring us happiness when each of us knows dozens of people who have all the things we seek, plenty of money, fast cars, good physical health, beautiful wives or handsome husbands, and still are miserable. Why do we not conclude therefrom that the two are not synonymous, and neither are they even in a cause and effect relationship. Similarly, all of us know or have heard of people who have renounced the things of this world, the things we seek, and who are infinitely happy. Why don't we draw the logical conclusion which flows inescapably from these observations and apply it to our own lives? Why do we not simply seek happiness, at its source (which is God), from the outset? And then if things like fast cars and beautiful spouses follow, well, good enough, and if not, good enough, because we'll be happy either way, which is what we wanted in the first instance. Why does each of us have to go the full gamut until it seems we own very nearly one of everything on earth, until finally, up to our ears in warehouse storage receipts, we seek for less and find the light? Can it be because each of us _is_ the One, and, there being no other, the One has to do it all, for Itself.

SURVIVAL

If survival is our principal or even only motivating factor, survival of "I" in this body and mind with all its memories and so on (which is what "I" is to the body/mind or ego), then all paradigms will be fashioned by that body/mind to ensure its survival. For example, consider the paradigms of after-life and of reincarnation: These may be the first tentative steps toward admitting that the body (at least as flesh) dies. "Yea, but, 'I' will survive!" is the immediate response."The mind that I believe myself to be will survive, even if the body doesn't." It is still egoic, and body/mind motivated. The "surviving" mind will fashion for itself some kind of new body, be it physical (in reincarnation) or ethereal (in after-life). The "mind" will survive and it will perceive its own survival in terms of or as a "body", however mortal or ethereal it may be to its perception. We still have not given up the concept of a separate body/mind.

Giving it _all_ up is so scary! Yet, in the final analysis, it is the only way to replace what we believe ourself to be, the body and its mind, with what we are in actuality, God being us! To realize _that_, "we" must die in all aspects of what we believe "we" are, and that includes all concepts of "I", "me", and "mine", including the "I" that continues after "death of the body". A vessel that is already full cannot be filled; we must be emptied to be refilled with God! Or, we cannot be unlimited or "think" in an unlimited manner, in wholeness (as God does), while maintaining a limited "I" paradigm, like _a_ body, _a_ mind, or _my_ body and _my_ mind, because that very limitation limits itself!

ALWAYS THE POOR

You will always have the poor, Jesus tells us. Why? Why did he not just wander about, and with a touch of his magic hands, enrich them all, for all time. Erase the problem with a flick of his wrist.

Is he perhaps telling us that so long as we live in the world there must always be manifested the full spectrum of every possibility, for the world is a reflection of (in the image of) God Which includes whatever there Is? Now, one hastens to note, that does not necessarily mean that there is poverty (or for that matter, wealth) in God, for in God there is nothing! But when one, in effect, pries out of God that nothing to get at something (that is, to experience one's self as a self other than other selves), one must accept all that comes with it, which is everything.

You see, God does not discriminate among His aspects. To Him, it is all One. "All of Me," He might croon to us, "Why not take all of Me?" Indeed, there is no other way to take Him except all at a time for He does not come piecemeal. After all, in an Infinite Being, Which is God, every aspect contains every aspect! So, wealth contains (or includes, or, ultimately, is) poverty; likewise, poverty is wealth. We perceive them as opposite extremes because that is what we are into, opposite extremes. That, after all, is how we know we exist, by the existence of others. Your existence confirms mine. I know I am me in part, if not entirely, by observing, or insisting, that I am not you. Just so, wealth informs or creates poverty. To know wealth, we must know poverty. Tall means nothing unless we also know what short means. Healthy is a meaningless concept without an understanding of illness.

You will always have the poor, Jesus said. Not, "there will

always be the poor," but "you will always have the poor". Who will? "You" will. Who are "you"? We are. Who are we? That is precisely the question. So long as we think of ourselves as selves other than other selves, there will always be, there must always be, others. So long as there are others, there will always be the poor. And the tall. And the skinny. And the opposite sex. And the foreigners. Others. Always others. To eliminate the poor, we must eliminate others. And to eliminate others, we must eliminate our selves.

"The Father and I are One," he said. No others.

The Father and I are <u>the</u> One.

THE APPEARANCE OF THINGS

The appearance of things rarely tells us the truth about something. We must look beyond or under the appearance to find the inner reality of something. This inner reality is seldom physically discernible, but instead is "felt" or "known", and consists of truth, or the <u>real</u> reality of life. It is God shining through His manifestations, or Himself manifesting. Often, in fact, the seemingly ugly appearance on the surface covers beauty within. And often, the seemingly beautiful appearance on the surface covers much sorrow, anger or "ugliness" within. (Of course, from God's point of view, nothing is ugly, even the seemingly ugly is beautiful. But from our point of view, humanly speaking, we look at things as opposites, and for this purpose, something opposite to beauty can be considered "ugly.") Thus, the physical is rarely a good indicator of inner states, much as we like to think so.

The problem here is the educated mind, or better, the cultured mind. Consider a child's mind. It is closer to God, closer than our minds, because it hasn't been educated into judgment or separation. It loves all things, including mud and dirt! This state of mind is what is meant by giving up everything for God or Christ. And that means literally everything. This includes all our learning, all our culture, all our cherished thoughts. Vacate the mind, and let God fill the vacancy. And He will. Giving up all material and learned thoughts seems an overwhelming sacrifice of great magnitude, but of course, it isn't a sacrifice at all. It is a release. It is freedom. It is the way home.

BEHAVE YOURSELF!

For my part, I find that remembering what it was like to be a child, how I ate, played, thought, learned, helps me to determine how to behave now. "Except ye be like little children..." is not a fairy tale, but a fact, and a promise.

WHO DIRECTS THE BEHAVIOR?

Who is it that I have given my authority to? My parents and their paradigms? My society and its paradigms? Indeed, do I give my authority to my own "belief system" which I hold now, uninspected, un-censored? Instead, I must give my authority to my true father and mother (God, the Universe), to my own inner authority (the Christ within). The problem is I have set my sights too low! I have been mimicking the lowest denominator and ignoring the highest. I have been accepting mediocrity, partly because of numbers, but mostly because of ignorance of my true nature. I have been looking down and out, instead of up and in.

THE EGO VERSUS GOD

How do I know whether the ego or God is urging me to do something, or is speaking through me? How do I know when it is God and not the ego-centric me?

If I want to "convert" others to my way of thinking, acting, behaving, be it taking dope or praying to God, it is ego directed. If, instead I am glad to show another my way, <u>if</u> he comes and asks, and in the event he doesn't do it quite my way, and I am left unmoved, then it is God directed. If I don't "care" about the outcome, then the ego isn't involved.

THE SENSE OF GOD

The sense of God is boundaryless, literally, and will often initially be attended by fear. You will not know where you are, you will feel as though you are everywhere all at once. Once experienced, and hopefully, not forgotten, you realize that bodily existence is simply by choice, and you can actually inhabit a multitude of bodies should you choose to. Then bodies become vehicles, simply and only that, nothing more. Body consciousness is confined, false, small, petty, indifferent, wrong, lost, blind, flat, broken, dumb, dark, heavy, small and isolated. Separate. God consciousness is expanded, universal, full, overflowing, all over the place, continuous, free, light, airy, un-wounded, warm and loving. Of course, in order to experience God "consciousness", the you that you believe yourself to be must cease. "You have only to die to Live."

A HORSE IS "HORSE-IER"

A horse is infinitely "horse-ier" than a dog, and a dog is infinitely "doggier" than a horse.

Do not compare what is, despite appearances, not comparable. People, things, events, and experiences may seem or appear to be the same or similar, but they are not. Each is uniquely itself, comparable to no other. So do not mumble "If only she were more like me," or "...this were more like that"; that can only lead to frustration and disappointment. Instead affirm, "I am glad she is as she is," even if you have to add sheepishly, "and I hope someday to understand why"!

I SEE MYSELF

The Great Teachers tell us: "I am God and I know that because I see Myself (God) expressed as you (us). I am the Light, and I know that because I see Myself (Light) reflected in you. Similarly, I am Love, and I know that because I see Myself (Love) radiating from you."

For our part, we say, "I am a fragile, frightened, separate mortal, and I know that because that is what I see in everyone else."

THE GONG SHOW

Consider this. The so-called subtle or etheric planes (the astral, the mental, the causal, and so on) all depend on the physical plane for their existence. That is, they are resonances or echoes of the physical. At so-called physical death, our point of focus or identity-awareness shifts from the physical to one of those planes, and we continue to exist "there" on the momentum we created or established in or as the physical plane, and we follow the direction or trajectory we established in or as the physical plane. Just as a rock that is thrown continues in the direction thrown even after having left the hand which threw it and until the throwing energy is expended.

Further, after so-called physical death, we continue in or as whatever subtle plane we have chosen for or as our point of focus only so long as the momentum or energy established in the physical remains. When that energy is used up or expended, we re-identify with or focus again at the physical level, in a procedure some call reincarnation, or resume the process all over again. Like a gong which, once struck, sends out sound waves; as they dissipate, we strike the gong again.

If any of this makes sense (and I am by no means altogether certain that it does) then it follows that the only way "out of" this process (if out is what we want, not to mention where "out" leads to!) is through the physical plane, because the other planes, whatever else we might say about them, are quite evidently only resonances or echoes of the original, the physical, of the gong which alone is the source of sound and therefore of the potential for silence. The only place to stop sending out sound waves is at the source of the noise, at the gong! Just so, if we were to shout out in a cave, any resounding echoes must follow after, and conform to, our original shout. The first echo and all the subsequent echoes cannot effect any changes to themselves; they cannot prolong or shorten their "life" span; they cannot raise or lower their key or frequency; they cannot alter any aspect of themselves. They are a slave to the original shout and depend absolutely on its nature, duration, and force, for their own. And to stop the echoing, at least any future echoing, the shouter not the echo must take action; that is, he must stop shouting.

Now, if we are the "shouters" or the gong-strikers in this equation, then the question becomes, do our lives here on the physical plane send out echoes or secondary waves which take their shape directly from our lives, from the kinds of people we choose to be and the kinds of choices about everything that we make? And are those echoes the planes we are destined to inhabit "after death"? If so, perhaps this very moment is a fine time to start sounding a little more pleasantly!

The body is the door by which we entered, and so the body must likewise be the door by which we exit.

DYING TO LIVE

God is not other. Not an other, not some other, not anything other. Specifically, God is not other than me (or you).

Knowing that (not just repeating it, but <u>knowing</u> it) may be what some traditions call God Realization. Whatever it's called, I want it. But, of course, the I who wants it is the same I who is standing in the way of my having it; that is, the I to whom God <u>is</u> an other. It is that I which must go so that I can see that He is not (not an other, that is). Which means I will never reach it; at least, not as the I that wants it.

So, eliminate the I that wants it, and I will have it. Thus, the Teachers insist, in order to live I must die.

Wait a minute. Perhaps there isn't a separate I that wants it, but only wanting. That is, maybe the wanting is the thing. Eliminate that and what's left? Having. After all, one who wants nothing, one who is without nothing, is by definition one who "has" everything. Including, presumably, God Realization.

That seems simple enough.

CONSIDERING DEATH

The only lasting way to overcome death is to die. By this I mean that the mortal, bodily human sense of individu-ality and separateness must be surrendered to God. Then death no longer exists because we will have truly recognized who we are, a being in and of God (a child of God, if you wish), not subject to death and change; and we, the separate, limited entity that we believe ourselves to be right now will have died at the same time, for all time.

The question to ask is: "Who is it that seeks to overcome death?" Is it our human sense of individuality, derived from identification with the body? For if so, we will never succeed. In the body's world, a world governed and created by thought, through the body, change is inevitable because thought is linear (moving from one idea to the next), and death is simply one of those changes, or ideas. Of course, we can put off death and prolong our lives by various mental processes or devices of thought, perhaps for many years, but eventually change must prevail and the body will die, because the body is of the "stuff" of thought, limited and time bound, and therefore cannot be eternal.

But if the answer to the question which asks "Who is it that seeks eternal life?" is the I AM, then that will indeed survive forever, because that is what God, the universe, everything, is, and who we are, and that will never die, just because it was never born. But to realize this state, to know the I AM that we are, you and I as separate entities must die. We cannot house two identities within us. Therefore one must be sacrificed to make room for, or to permit expression of, the other. If we wish to be eternal, then our short-term identity, the one that is born and therefore will die, the identity of the body, is the one that must go, or die.

DEATH IS LIFE, AND LIFE IS DEATH

Perhaps we have it backwards, as usual. What we think of as life on earth in ego-centric terms, is really death, and in death, either voluntarily or involuntarily (willful relinquishment of the ego, or old-age death), we find actual Life. Death is not the enemy, but the friend. Think about it. Who is it that is afraid of death? The ego, the separative self. Who keeps us living on earth, at all costs? The ego, the separative self. What is it that is most afraid of what we might learn at death? The ego, the separative self. Why? Because we will know that without the ego, what's left, what's real, is God! And without the ego, the sense of separation that makes the ego seem real, we will no longer be separated from God, and will <u>be</u> of and in God. Of course, we do not see this until we permit ourselves to, for the ego continues so long as we nourish it - - God is <u>so</u> gracious. But still the truth observed here remains the truth: Death in all its forms, physical and spiritual, is always the friend, because when death occurs, expansion occurs with it, and thus we come closer to God. If this whole idea seems disturbing, perhaps an understanding of the term "death" is in order. Death means final and terminal ending of some state, <u>in exchange</u> for another, for we are eternal. Only for those of us who don't know we are eternal, does death become fearful.

WHAT'S HE WANT ANYWAY?

God wants it <u>all</u>, not part of it.

BORED TO DEATH

Physical death is an indulgence to the body experience. It is a decision taken at some level within us not to remain in the body, or no longer to manifest the body, but nonetheless to continue of the body. In that sense, all death is suicide. Perhaps it may be prompted by a sense of boredom, frustration, or fear; or it may simply be a reach for distraction, or the logical expression of the conclusion that we have done what we chose to do this time around. But whatever the case, death is not an escape from the physical. On the contrary, it is an endorsement or reaffirmation of the physical. After all, death of the body is, by definition, of the body. We can accept the reality of physical death only if we accept the reality of the physical body.

Thus, death does not free us of the body's regime any more than moving from Maine to California frees us from Washington's authority. It is a change of environment, offering a whole range of new experiences in an altogether different set of circumstances, but it is still of the same order of things. As many would have it, death is indeed "the other side"; but the other side of the same old thing, of the physical. To escape that, it is not enough to die in the body. We must die to the body. To escape the physical, we must transcend the physical.

Jesus said that if we wish to live we must die. As it is clear from his teachings that he is talking about spiritual life, or Life, so is it clear that he is not talking about physical death. It is not enough to die physically in order to be reborn spiritually. To die physically simply facilitates or permits being reborn physically, here or somewhere else. To be reborn spiritually we must first die to the physical. Before we can answer the question "Whose death?", we must answer the question,

"Who do I think I am?" If the answer to that was born, then it will die, sooner or later, probably from boredom.

BORED TO DISTRACTION

Despite popular belief to the contrary, boredom is not having nothing to do. Boredom is the desire for distraction. Thus, the solution to boredom is not to find something to do, because it is inevitable that whatever activity we undertake will eventually get done, restoring us once again to boredom, at least until we gin up something else to do. In that regime, we sentence ourselves to a lifetime career as our own "cruise director", eternally condemned to having to think of things to keep ourselves busy, active and distracted.

The answer is to release the desire for distraction. Free of that we will never again be bored.

COME DIE WITH ME

If I could only die every moment of my life then I would live constantly without memory and without expectations. Think of it: literally starting afresh every single moment of our lives. Without any prejudices or judgments, without any sense of having to fulfill the desires, real or perceived, of others, without any preconceived notions about how we or others ought to live.

Being always reborn and newborn, I could address every moment as my first; fresh, clean, and free, as if nothing had gone before. Unconditional awareness.

Now, that's dying. That's love.

LOOK AT ME

When God looks at me (and you, and you, and you) He sees Himself.

In fact, that is the only way God can see Himself: as me (and you, and you, and you).

Indeed, one might say that that is what we are, God's reflection. God seeing Himself. Created "in His image", we are God imaging God. That may be our only function: to provide God a means of seeing and knowing Himself.

"Look at me," God exclaims, looking at me (and you, and you, and you), "Aren't I beautiful!"

FREE TO DIE

Surely karma is simply memory. And to forgive is simply to give up or release every event or experience totally or absolutely <u>in advance</u>, not only as it happens but even before it happens, thus avoiding or eliminating the accumulation of memory and escaping the karmic re-birth cycle.

Consider it this way. Karma is the generation or the reincarnation of memory, which is thought in the past tense. Thought as memory takes form again, or comes to life again, every time we recall it. Just as we can "relive" last year's vacation trip to Yosemite by dragging out the old slides, so too will we eventually relive or reincarnate the events or experiences, the thoughts, of our lives if we take them with us "to the grave". Those thoughts will linger so long as we nourish them by keeping them alive in memory, awaiting an opportunity to manifest anew, awaiting our reach for the slide projector and screen, awaiting reformation which some call reincarnation. But if we can be free of those thoughts, clear of all memories, then there will be nothing left to take form. We will be free, free to die.

Thus, we must learn to die cleanly, without any accompanying baggage. Perhaps the easiest way to do that is to die often, even every moment, before we have a chance to begin accumulating thoughts, memories, slides. So, whatever it is that is on your mind now, do what needs to be done and then let go of it, release it quickly and cleanly before it takes on your life.

WHEN THE EGO DIES

Now that we know that the cause of all the misery is the ego (the sense that we are separate entities, disconnected and isolated from the "rest" of the world), and that to reach transcendence or God, the ego has but to die, how do we go about accomplishing? What can we do, if anything, to help facilitate or speed the progress? This desired transcendence is ultimately inevitable, anyway, but presumably only through centuries and centuries of work. For those of us who are impatient, or have had enough of this struggle, what can we do to hurry it along?

In my personal experience, it seems to me that there are only two things we can do. One is to surrender it all. Go to a higher source, to God, or who or whatever we wish to call the supreme power that created all "this", and release ourself totally, absolutely to Him. With surrender comes the loss or the release of everything we consider "mine" and "me". Through that relinquishment, the death of the ego, which is based upon the concept of "me" and "mine", occurs, obviously. It is the simplest, and yet also the most difficult way, for some of us.

For those of us who cannot (or will not) surrender, there is another option. There is a process of inattention which will work equally as well, though perhaps with more internal struggle. Simply through inattention to the "things" of the ego, we can facilitate its death. In other words, by turning our attention to non-ego subjects (which, when thoroughly considered, leaves only God!), the ego, from lack of attention to its things, and by extension, to itself, will simply wither away and die. By lack of attention, I mean simply that. By turning our attention to transcendence, to non-ego concepts (if there is such a thing!), the creative faculty of the mind lessens its hold on the things of the ego, and in time, through this inattention, brings about the end of the ego. In effect, we cease "feeding" the ego. It dies of starvation. This, in turn, brings about the death of "me" and "mine", and ultimately the death of all separative sense. While on paper this sounds simple, and in theory it is, the actual practice, at least initially, is very difficult. This is precisely because we have been trained to serve the ego, conditioned to attend to its many desires, and the change of consciousness required cannot occur without pain of some kind, emotional, mental, or physical. However, it _can_ be accomplished, and is being accomplished, and with determination and aspiration, it will be won. These seem to be two ways to transcend the mind, if that is what we wish to do, or course!

All the ego is, is thought, created by the desires, senses and needs of the body and its mind. Ego depends on thought for its very existence.

If this is so, then if we stop thought, through some mechanism or other, then the ego will disappear, right? And alternatively, if we restart thought, the ego reappears. Now, when thought stops (as in deep meditation, dreamless sleep, other trance-like states, or moments of stillness), we continue to exist, do we not? Obviously we do, we all do, all the time! Then, we have to ask ourselves, during those times when thought stops but we still exist, what is it that is still existing? What is it that is behind, over and above, transcendent to the ego and its thoughts?

Of course, each of us must answer this for ourselves from within; no one can tell us, because the telling is the activity of thought, and is thus one ego telling another ego about something which an ego cannot know. But this real me or real you exists nonetheless. Something, which is me or you exists during these times of ego absence. Of course, by extension, this "something" always exists, even during times of thought, as it is beyond and transcendent to thought. And whatever it is, it is obviously not dependent upon thought (the ego) for its existence. Perhaps we can at least say, albeit with words and thought, that the ego is really just a superimposition on the real me or the real you. That is a good place to begin, for it provides us with a potent weapon against the huge odds of a" world" founded upon and supported by thought and ego. And, if we follow on from that starting place, it will take me and you to God!

HOW CAN I KNOW

How can I know that Thou art me,
So long as I think that I am?

How can I know that I am Thee,
So long as I think that I am me?

How can I know that I am,
    if I am not?
How can I know which I knows,
    and which I isn't?

How will I know that I know when I know?

Once, a dentist, applying an anesthetic, said, "Let me know when you can no longer feel this." How will I know that I am not feeling it when I can no longer feel it?

GIVE HIM WHAT YOU WANT

What God wants from us is our identity (so that He can give us His in exchange).

Remember, identity comes from the Latin word meaning "the same as"; that is, what do we think we are "the same as"? If we have given our identity to another, or accepted the identity of another - - be it a person, a club, a nation, or whatever - - then we have first to retrieve or reassert it, so that we can offer it to God. Clearly, we cannot give to God what we have given to another. So, first we must affirm: I am somebody; in and of myself, I matter. I do not need you to be me; it is enough to be me. I love being me. Then, just before it becomes distracting and habit-forming, we give that healthy identity, that one we love, ourselves, to God. And He turns it into Himself.

So, the only way to get what we want is to give Him what He wants, because ultimately, whether we know it or not, that <u>is</u> what we want.

Think of <u>transcending</u> as "trance ending", as in the end of sleep, or awakening.

Thus, we transcend the world not by sprouting wings but by opening our eyes.

THE MYSTERY OF DISEASE

Why is it that enlightened masters, the great teachers of metaphysics, the greatest of saints, all die, all have diseases of some sort, and yet all claim that there is no disease and no death? And why is it that often all the mental affirmations, prayers, and positive work in the world do not heal a body, despite the promise from these same masters and teachers that that sort of work will do so?

There seems to be a contradiction, a paradox of enormous proportion here, and as this obvious fact is staring at me and I cannot deny it, then the fault must be in my judgment or understanding of the paradox, not in the teachings of the facts themselves. It must be my concept of "perfection" as well as "health" that is at fault. It must be my consciousness or my understanding of "mind" that is incorrect, as these promises are not made lightly, nor are they made by dishonest beings. I must admit that the human mind, upon which I depend so greatly, is limited, capable of enormous distortion and misunderstanding, because I cannot escape the fact that it cannot solve this seeming paradox by logic alone. Rather, I have to come to this problem through a change in consciousness, a release of separative thought.

First, the "mind" that affirms and "creates" health is not the same mind that affirms healing because of fear of disease. The affirming mind of a great saint or master is a mind which is no longer "theirs". They simply have no will of their own, and in fact their "minds" are continuously on God, their consciousness of God's, and whatever remains of their own "mind" is constantly submerged and surrendered to their source, God. That is why their prayers work, and mine often don't. When mine do, it is in fact only when I have forgotten myself long enough to allow God's consciousness to work its miracles. The fault lies not in the promise, but in my own limited application of the promise.

Hearing what the masters truly have to say, we discover that health, as we describe it (a physical body without evidence of decay, degeneration or discomfort) has little if anything to do with health as defined from the perspective of God, which includes everything, including ill health! The body which is born and which dies is ultimately not all of me, or anybody. Health is actually a state of purity, peacefulness, sanctity and holiness. It has nothing to do with the physical world but everything to do with our state of consciousness. We have chosen to ignore what the saints have said all along. We are not the body nor the body's mind, the limited, time space continuum of stuff, but the stuff of God. With this discovery, we are no longer limited to or subject exclusively to the rules and regulations of a material universe and world. However, to the extent that we identify with the material universe and world, so will our ideas of death and disease be molded. By embracing God's consciousness, the manifestations of the body and its mind become secondary, if not unimportant in every sense. If we are fully conscious of being consciousness itself, beyond and including all body stuff and mind, then whatever occurs within that frame of reference is inconsequential, just as a stubbed toe is inconsequential to my own current state of body consciousness, or a dying cell (of which there are millions moment to moment in my body all the time) goes unnoticed, unheeded and of no concern to my integrity as a being.

Thus, what is it to a being who is all encompassing, is all beings, is all the stuff of the universe, that one of its multitudes of bodies dies or appears to suffer? Do I feel my suffering dying cells as they "meet their maker"? Not at all! I am, in fact, unaware of the occurrence! And yet I am left fully intact! This same state of consciousness applies to the being who knows who he is, to the being who is no longer bound or identifies with his body and its mind, but instead identifies with and knows that he *is* the universe, and beyond the universe! Thus disease, from the standpoint of an all-embracing, non-exclusive being, becomes nothing other than a bacterial transformation of matter, a necessary event in the transformative action of nature, an inevitable conclusion to that which is born. Do not forget, once we know ourselves to be consciousness, not body bound, not time or space bound, that that consciousness is neither born, nor dies. And thus we have eternal life, we *are* eternal life or immortality. Because you and I (as that consciousness) are not born, therefore, neither can we die, it is simply impossible!

Now, none of the foregoing is intended to suggest that enlightened beings, or any being motivated by unselfish love, cannot or do not physically heal others, for of course they can and do, all the time. However, I believe that these healings are accomplished simply though compassion (which is ultimately loving consciousness!), and not through any belief on their part (at least in the case of enlightened beings) that it is "better" to be "healthy" physically than non-healthy. This can be substantiated by the observation that, when it comes to their own physical health, they invariably say that they do not care and that their body's state of health is of no consequence to them whatsoever. Of course, to those of us who are so afraid of ill health and identify with that frail, limited body, their apparently careless attitude seems madness or, at best, highly contradictory. At the least, it doesn't fit with our paradigm of what we think is perfect, and of what we think we are. We have become so intent on "getting" or maintaining "health", or "happiness", and so on, that we don't even know what the words really mean, let alone how to achieve any of it, if in fact there is actually any achievement involved!

In the final analysis, all we "get" is God, and all that is worth "getting" is God. Thus, happiness is simply letting go and letting myself, whatever that is, be merged with and consumed by God consciousness, to the extent possible for me. And that "letting go" certainly does not include "wealth", as I thought I understood it, "health" as I thought I understood it, or for that matter, "happiness" as I conceived it to be in the form of pleasure and non-suffering. We simply do not understand the meaning of what it is to be in any of these states from the point of view of God, and will not until such time as we are IT. That can only come through forgetting who it is that we <u>think</u> we are and letting God instruct us in (or transform us into) what we <u>actually</u> are.

Finally, we again come to the fact that we cannot put our attention on two things at once, and if we are pursuing anything other than God, then we are not pursuing God, and ultimately, that is all we <u>are</u> and all we <u>want</u>.

ABOUT HEALING

If one is to be a healer, one must be healed. And to be healed, one must be "diseased" in one way or another in order to have something to heal. We cannot give up what we don't have, and we also cannot understand or explain a process unless we have experienced it ourselves. It cannot be truly taught otherwise. Knowledge, the real kind, is lived, not learned through the mere repetition of another's thoughts.

In the process of healing, how is it that one can know he is healed and yet still be manifesting sickness through his body? I think this is what happens when change occurs in thought. With a correction in thinking, in the sense of thinking Godly thoughts as opposed to ego-centric thoughts (which ultimately leads to non-thought), there are many corrections of thinking that occur concurrently. As each cleansing thought purifies a body that has previously reflected incorrect thinking, there manifest rashes, aches and pains, headaches, colds, whatever. Depending on the severity and tenacity of the old thinking, the adjustment to corrected or "higher" thinking may well cover years, and may likely come in increments. A lot of healing has to do with patience.

In the process of healing, as one corrects one's thinking, there is no reason that the expression of these changes must be discordant, inharmonious or painful. However, the process of change will have to be expressed. It will have to rise to the surface, and the resistance to this may cause more discomfort than the original complaint! Often, our fear of the transforming process going on within us itself creates more problems and symptoms, symptoms which we interpret as new or renewed disease! But simple common sense tells us that as changes occur in the mind, so they will be manifested and expressed through the body. Therefore, one can rightly say it is merely "Kundalini activity", or better, "it is simply realignment with God". When a car is realigned, there occurs a shift, a settling and a creaking of the body into the new alignment, an adjustment into the new position. The process requires physical movement from the old direction to the new. Thus, getting back to human bodies, one might suggest that in a certain sense chiropractors are actually trying to accomplish physically what must be done mentally!

In the process of being healed, one must learn meekness. This may be the only reason that God would permit sickness to be allowed to be prolonged in the body of an otherwise healed being. When meekness is learned, disease is no longer useful to a seeker's unfoldment. Of course, this does not apply to the cases of Masters who are either teaching something through sickness, or who simply take no notice of the body or its condition, and thus no longer care if the body (which is no longer them, and never was) is well or sick.

Often we cannot understand why a disease will not go away despite the many prayers, inner work, etc., that we do. While God does not <u>cause</u> disease, He will use whatever is available to draw us closer to Him. (Or, depending on our perspective, we will use whatever is available to draw us closer to our inner Self.) Read Job in the Bible if you don't believe this! Also, note in Job that God didn't <u>cause</u> the disease, but <u>permitted</u> Satan to cause it. (On the other hand, how much difference is there between "cause" and "permit", particularly as regards an omnipotent being?!) If we are self-righteous, not humble, not meek, but judgmental, whatever, and because of these traits invite disharmony that displays itself in the form of disease, then perhaps God will "permit" our discomfort in order to get our attention. If the condition does not abate, perhaps we might ask ourselves what disharmony of thought may be continuing the situation, or what it is we are to learn here.

To run from sickness simply because of the discomfort it causes us, may miss the point of it, and thus will not heal us, or bring us closer to God in any way.

A serious disease which enforces reclusiveness may well be a result of a drastic change in thought, a drastic realignment of perspective. The disharmony produced by this kind of change can create inner confusion in which so-called "good" or healing thoughts conflict with old, "bad" alignment. And the adjustment process takes time.
In other words, disharmony is not always bad! Sometimes it is a symptom of healing. In any change from one position to another, there is bound to be a period of disharmony, or discomfort, but

all while we are on our way towards a better alignment. And enforced reclusiveness caused by discomfort or physical handicap may be necessary to the process, and in fact a kindness to the seeker, who perhaps now needs a large doese of silent time to understand the change in progress and to integrate it into his life. If he tries to continue as he did before, if he tries to maintain the "status quo", he will not have the time necessary for this integration to occur, or the time to see the revelations that accompany it. Thus, we must allow our outer lives to reflect what is going on inwardly, and if we struggle against that adjustment, it may be forced upon us, ultimately for our own good, even if at the price of considerable discomfort and fear.

OBEDIENCE TRAINING

A dull blade is worse than no blade. Likewise, a dull mind is a useless and dangerous tool.

Concentration is the process by which the mind, the seat of reason, is honed, eventually to a keen edge, so that, sharp and quick as a warrior's sword, it can cut neatly to the core, discarding the rind, exposing the fruit. Thus, it is by concentration that we get to the Truth; not that we know it, but that we reveal its source.

When, by practised concentration, the instrument is dependable and in good working order, the mind is encouraged and confidently undertakes its struggle with Truth. Emboldened by its new found strength and locked in the fight of its life, reason wrestles the Supreme, Love, ultimately to win by losing, drowned in the all-consuming awareness that what seemed never was and what is is, in a word, unreasonable. Long and dark, this is not an easy time. One after another, old friends and familiar crutches fall by the way, and we are left alone, naked, standing, falling, kneeling, crying. Until finally, the vessel emptied and cleansed, we are refilled. By Him. In Him. As Him.

As for the rest, it cannot be described and will not be spoken, for no language contains it. In the words of Jesus, "Where I am, you cannot come." Not because it is a private club with exclusive, restrictive membership requirements ("Male Christian Saints Only"), but because where he is there is room enough only for One, and so long as you and I think of ourselves as you and I, well, two is two too many.

So, to get there, we go back to basics, to obedience training, to learning concentration. We learn to sit. And to stay.

WILL

There is will and there is Will. One is of God, the other of man. Will acting passively is Will, of God. Will acting aggressively is will, of man.

DISCIPLINE

Before discipline of action must come discipline of thought and <u>always</u> discipline of emotion.

ALONG THE WAY

There is enormous fear, terrible struggle, and great, great difficulty in learning new ideas and letting go of old. Despite the overwhelming longing to do it, despite even the commitment to change, it is very hard!

WILLFULNESS VERSUS GOD-THOUGHT

Willfulness interferes with, indeed prevents, God-Thought from entering our lives, our hearts. By willfulness, I mean insistence on the part of a separative, individual mind to express and impose itself (its will) upon the world it interacts with. This is willfulness. The will, however, can be <u>used</u> by the separative, individual mind to <u>turn</u> itself to God and to surrender, thereby using its will to <u>allow</u> or invite God-Thought to infiltrate that mind, and thereby, eventually to win the heart.

God-Thought is a self-contradictory term. Thought, as we know it, does not occur within the context of God-Thought. First, it is not an activity, nor is it linear, in the sense that our thoughts are. It is non-dual, and unitive, whole. However, it is "thought" in that it is consciousness, awareness, beingness, and is "perceived" by my mind, but only after the fact, not during. It is easy to see, then, how willfulness can interfere with God-Thought, as the two forms of "perception" do not accomodate each other, in fact, they cancel each other out!

Finally, it comes down to what I want. My will, or His! The two obviously cannot coexist. Clearly, though, the choice is mine! Interesting, isn't it, that in a universe created by an all-knowing God, the choice to "know" this was left up to a <u>non</u>-all-knowing entity. If you chew on this for a while, willfulness seems to evaporate.

RELIGION AND TRUTH

It seems to be the function of religion in most cultures to explain and regulate life in this world. Religion tells us what we can and cannot do, how we are to do it, with whom, and under what circumstances, and what will happen if we don't. Thus, although it might seem from some of its language to be mostly other-worldly, religion is actually pretty much this-worldly. Now, this is not necessarily a bad thing, and the observation is not made here as a negative criticism. Rather, it is offered simply as something to be aware of as through life we march along.

According to virtually all the Teachers, it seems to be the function of Truth that it liberates us from this world. (Actually, that might be better stated, "... to be the nature of Truth that it liberates us from this world," because Truth does not really have a function; it simply is.) In fact, they say, Truth is not of this world. Thus, it would seem that religion and Truth are at odds. The one is focused on regulating our behavior in this world and the other on freeing us from it.

Ordinarily, this realization might disturb us, contradicting as it seems to do so much of what we have been brought up to believe. But when we recall that Truth, being God, is Infinite and therefore includes everything everywhere, we are reassurred that religion too, being something somewhere, is included within Truth and therefore also serves Truth.

For us, perhaps the important lesson here is to recognize that the one is not precisely the other, and to remember to distinguish between the two when we or others speak of them.

THE WORD RELIGION

According to my dictionary, the origin of the word <u>religion</u> is "uncertain". Curious.

I remember reading somewhere that the traditional or orthodox view, at least as regards the so-called Judeao-Christian culture, is that the word comes from the Latin <u>religare</u>. That is particularly interesting because that root has all to do with binding and tying, and some might make, indeed some have made, a very strong case that it has in fact been the effect if not the function of orthodox religion to bind and tie. Perhaps knowing that is why the dictionary's publishers, being presumably of the "establishment" and thus mostly more orthodox, chose to conclude that the origin of the word is "uncertain". It might have been seen as singularly unwise to announce to the world that the root function of religion is not, as it professes, to free the world, but to bind and tie it.

Now, there is another Latin word which others point to as a more likely root of our word religion, and that is <u>relegere</u>. This word has a very different meaning from the other. <u>Relegere</u> means "to bring together again", as in, shall we say, to re-join or re-unite what has been put asunder. Religion defined from this perspective might be understood as serving to free the world, or perhaps more accurately, to free us of the world. To permit and facilitate the reunion of Father and Son.

Of course, which root we choose to follow, <u>religare</u> or <u>relegere</u>, will be determined by what we believe about ourselves and what we hope to accomplish by the religious process. Unfortunately, as we have in effect one word with two meanings, we are bound to mislead and confuse one another, unintentionally or otherwise, as we converse on this subject, but at least by having flagged the problem here, we can stop confusing ourselves!

RELIGION SEEKS WHAT LIBERATION FINDS

Religion seeks to fill our need for security, happiness, a sense of identity, comfort in times of distress, certainty in times of frustration and fear, and so on, and inevitably it must ultimately fail. Partly it fails because by seeking to fill these needs it constantly reasserts their validity. "Come to me for protection from the rain," besides promising to keep my head dry reinforces my belief that I need protection from the rain. Also, it puts me into a permanent dependent relationship. To keep dry I have to stay under religion's roof, and then I am no longer free to roam the universe at will. Further, I have to be alert to leaks in the roof, and be willing to repair them, not to mention punish those who cause them. Too, needs, like desire, are insatiable and infinite; the more they are fed, the hungrier they get. And, God knows, they breed like rabbits; once you encourage one by seeking to fill it, it splits into another, endlessly.

Liberation frees us from our needs by denying them. Now, by that is most certainly not meant repressing them or ignoring them, for that serves nothing. Denying them means acknowledging, finally and probably for the first time ever, that we are not what we think we are, not what our well-intentioned-and-loving parents and culture have taught us that we are, but instead what God says that we are, and what every Teacher of God has said that we are, since the beginning. God has no needs, for being Infinite God is and therefore has all there is. Created in His image, we are like Him. In every respect!

The choice offered to us here then seems to be: Would we prefer to have our needs filled and be dependent upon that source of fulfillment for all time, or would we rather be without needs and therefore free?

As for me, give me freedom.

THE USES AND ABUSES OF DOCTRINE

Once we have learned what we came to learn, it is time to move on. While this applies to our lives generally, it also applies specifically with regard to doctrine.

Doctrine can be stifling, because it is set and dogmatic. Doctrine can be useful, in that it can teach the lesson we came to learn, but <u>never</u> embrace the doctrine of another as absolute and not open to discussion, no matter how high sounding and elevated it may be. It is always limited, simply because it has been interpreted and expressed through the mind of an individual, or individuals, and is therefore limited, to some extent at least, by their paradigms and prejudices. However, the truth behind it can be liberating for us as students of that doctrine. But, the lesson of truth is the only important aspect within that doctrine, and once learned, we <u>must</u> move on to other "doctrines," with of course the same attitude towards that doctrine as the one we recently left.

TO LIVE BY FAITH

To live by faith we must have the following virtues; courage, waitfulness, watchfulness, expectancy, patience, surrender, lack of willfulness, trust, listening, and hope.

THE ONLY BEGOTTEN SEA

Consider the globe as seen from space. Besides the lakes and other land-locked areas of water, there is only one sea, one body of blue. To be sure, we talk of the Seven Seas, of the Atlantic Ocean, the Caribbean Sea, the Persian Gulf, and so forth, but all of that is just make-believe. Those are simply names which we have assigned to the one sea, the one body which we have arbitrarily carved up into geographical bits and territorial pieces. If you doubt it look at the globe again. There is only one sea and there only ever was.

Think about that. One sea, one virtually infinite body of water, equally ocean everywhere, washing up simultaneously and similarly on every shore without discrimination or distinction. Were it to speak it might proclaim, "Behold, I am the Sea, and beside Me there is no other." Just imagine. Then, each of us, upon hearing those words spoken at our shores, might join with neighbors who also heard and are now chanting with fervor,

"Yea, yea, this is the Sea, our sea,
Which has spoken to us, saying,
Ours alone is the Sea, and
All others are not."

And those who live on other shores who also heard the Sea speak that day from their own beaches, we will ridicule, or shun, or destroy. Rape their women, steal their gold, burn their beachhouses. Singing, "Yea, yea, ours alone is the Sea, and all others are not."

All the while, the one Sea continues to wash up similarly and simultaneously on every shore, without discrimination or distinction, cleansing the blood and rinsing the tears we shed in its name. And all the while it continues to sing to those who will hear,

> "Behold, I am the Sea,
> The only begotten Sea."

WHEN AN ACORN IS NOT AN ACORN

Consider this. If an acorn insisted on remaining an acorn, then the sprouting process would be perceived as awful, anticipated with dread, and experienced as pain. But suppose that instead the acorn perceived itself not as a thing but as the process of "tree-ing" (or, to be more accurate, "oaking") seen or captured in time, like a snapshot of one moment in a continuing series of moments. Thus, identifying with the whole, with the process of growth itself, it would lose all sense of fear which formerly attended each change, for it would know that change is virtually synonymous with growth, and growth is what it is. Perceiving itself as the process rather than as the thing processed would change everything.

Seeing ourselves as the process rather than as the thing processed <u>does</u> change everything.

RELIGION IS, LOVE IS

Religion is a creation of man to appease the thing he fears most, which is God.

Love is an expression of God to reach the thing He loves most, which is us.

Religion is a group undertaking, perhaps because we believe there is safety in numbers. "While it is unlikely He will believe me or spare me," we think, "perhaps if I remain in the crowd, at least He won't notice me!"

Love, on the other hand, is always one-on-one. That, of course, is why the prospect of it frightens us so fiercely, because we feel so inadequate alone. One, we think, is the most vulnerable number there is, when, in fact, One is the only number there is.

Until we love, we need religion, to give us courage in our fears. Once we love, we need nothing, because we know that love, which we are, is all there is.

All for You! Only for You!

LET THE WATERS

We hear a report on the television evening news about a boatload of refugees who are washed overboard and then attacked, and eaten, by several schools of sharks. We are overwhelmed. How could God permit such an outrage! Then, an hour or so later, in prime time, we watch a program about several boatloads of fishermen working a school of tuna, hauling them aboard by hook and grapple. We are elated. Thank you, Father, we exclaim with reverence, for Thy bounty.

Why aren't we as horrified at the killing of tuna by humans as we are at the killing of humans by sharks? Obviously because we <u>are</u> humans. Fair enough, I suppose. But how dare we expect that God will share our grief over the one and not grieve the other? Where does it say God is on our side and not the sharks', or the tuna's? Why, in our Bible, of course. Yes, our Bible: written by humans, about humans, for humans. How do we know that sharks don't have a Bible? And what might it say about us? How do we know that tuna don't have an evening news? God help us if they do!

How egocentric we are. Is there any hope? I wonder.

Seeing myself in all beings,
And all beings in myself,
I illuminate the entire Universe with love,
And I am so illuminated.

A PARADIGM OF SIN

Consider the Fall this way. The Fall, in the Garden of Eden, was actually self-consciousness of the creative power. In other words, originally, all beings (which were actually of and in God) were in fact being God, or God being beings, created <u>as</u> God, or better, as God through Himself as beings. We, or Adam and Eve in this instance, were innocent of this creative power, despite the fact that they (or, again, we) were creating <u>as</u> God. They were not self-conscious, not reflecting self will. In their innocence, they were in "heaven". The serpent (self-consciousness) introduced (subtley) the concept of self-creative power, "knowledge" of self (the tree), and the ability, already residing within, of creation with self-will. According to the King James version of the Bible, the serpent said, "you shall be as gods". Notice the use of the plural here. Not as God, but as many gods. In other words, the creative power is ours, <u>either</u> as God, or as gods. Here is the problem, and the Fall. As gods, there is conflict, because there is plurality, more than one, and multitudes, difference. As God, there is one, unitive, non-conflicting, heavenly!

WE ARE WHO I AM

As God is everywhere, in and as everything that is, it is obviously true that there is no one who is closer to God than anyone else, and no one to whom God is more easily or readily accessible than any other. Just as there can be no degrees of infinity (as in, "more" infinite or "less" infinite), so that which is Infinite (God) cannot be more here or there than there or here. Likewise, it (God) cannot be closer to, or farther from, here or there, cannot be more in you than in me, or, let's say, more in Jesus or the Buddha than in me or you. What is infinite is equally everywhere always.

So, the only difference between those two and you and me is that they <u>know</u> this (and thus are wholly comforted by their constant Presence in God), and you and I are still struggling to convince ourselves of it (and thus live in the shadow of fear).

But at least we can take heart from the recognition that the difference is more apparent than real, and therefore cannot truly threaten us, however terrifying its image may seem from time to time.

Eventually, all the Teachers assure us, you will see it as I do, because you are Who I AM.

Thank God.

JESUS SAVES

Jesus did not come to free us but to tell us that we are already free. Thus, he is not a savior (that is, one who saves), but a reminder (one who reminds). Or, if you prefer, a messenger. Our confusion over the past two thousand years (and it is a confusion shared equally by other cultures as regards other reminders) has been that we look to the messenger to perform for us the feat which only the message can accomplish, and that only by our proper understanding and application of it. You see, to effect this Message, we must become it, just as he had to become it in order to deliver it. (How else except in practice does the message "You are free" have meaning?)

Thus, Jesus tells us in effect, "I am not He Who sent me, but I am he whom He sent. I am the Message." This after having spent thirty years or so (the so-called "lost years") out of sight, unloading and renouncing, cleansing and purifying, so that the Message, always Pure, could be delivered Purely. Having received the Message, Jesus had to become it; having become it, he delivered it (by being it). The next link in that series might have been, "having had it delivered, we received it." But there it bogged down. We wanted him to throw out the Romans (or the Russians), or make us millionaires (or whatever), because that's what we think being free is all about.

In a word, Jesus became Christ the instant he knew that he was free. Or, he knew that he was Christ the instant he saw that he was free. He showed himself to us that we could see what we are. Failing absolutely to understand, we killed what we thought he was, and accomplished nothing. Having been there himself, Jesus was not the least bit surprised by our behavior. When someday we stop, and see, neither will we be.

GOOD AND BAD ENERGY

There is no "good" or "bad" energy, in the sense that we use these terms. We <u>are</u> energy, and it manifests or we permit ourselves to manifest, either flowingly or haltingly. When the energy is stopped from flowing the results <u>appear</u> to be bad, or aberrant, <u>because</u> it is no longer flowing; but in and as itself, it is neither "good" nor "bad". Sometimes, energy can flow so strongly and intensely that it causes seeming disease. In fact, it "burns out" the body. This might be called "good disease."

THE CREATIVE PART

The creative part of man is in his hands, they mold and create, do they not? Notice where they emanate from. The heart. Therefore, where is it that all healing, creation, and "molding" originate, certainly not in the head! Find out what the heart signifies and you find out what, and where, God's "mind" is, and concurrently, who you are.

OM OR AUM

Have you ever noticed the extraordinary similarity in sound, and spelling, between Om or Aum, and I Am? This strikes me as highly significant, especially in light of the Bible's repeated references to the I Am as God, and Hinduism's reverence for the sound of the Universe, Om or Aum, and our repeated use of the word I Am in reference to ourselves. Perhaps there is a clue here as to what, and how, we should meditate? Hmmmmmmm?!

WHAT IS AN ENLIGHTENED BEING?

An enlightened being is unlimited being that knows it has become limited (this limitation occuring either willfully, or through the usual process of nature), and continues to exist as a limited being for the sake of all other unenlightened beings.

FROM THE HEART

From the heart, imagine yourself physically falling into the arms of God. Fall as often as possible. That is what surrender feels like, initially.

GOING YOUR WAY?

If the rest of the world seems to be going in the same direction you are, chances are you're headed the wrong way.

This spiritual undertaking is not a journey for the multitudes but for one. The gate is narrow not because some will be excluded, but because all are excluded. That is, it is wide enough to permit passage only one by one. Thus, wherever you're going, if you're in a crowd, leave the crowd. Be yourself, you and God alone.

Look directly to God, one-on-one. That is the only relationship God understands, for One is as far as God can count.

There is no way we can live truly free in "this world" because, in some inexplicable sense, this world does not exist except as a symptom of the disease we all suffer from and call life. Seeking peace in the context of the world is like a fever victim looking for a home in the environment of his hallucinations, or a desert traveler seeking to quench his thirst in the water of a mirage, or a prisoner painting an open door on the wall of his cell.

There is no way out but out.

THE OBJECT OF LIFE

The object of life is <u>not</u> to ... be happy, be healthy, enjoy great wealth, make love, make war, have a baby, have a ball, drive fast, fly high, or anything else that we might think or pray for.

The object of life is to be.

Thus, no one else can "do it" for us, whatever the "it" might be, because the object is not that it get done (although our goal-oriented belief structure has great difficulty seeing that), but rather that we, whoever we are, participate fully, unreservedly, and without prejudice in the doing of it.

It is very much like teaching and learning. A teacher, however bright and dedicated, cannot learn for a student. It would totally defeat the purpose of the educational system were he or she, however charitably motivated, to attempt to do so.

Perhaps if we would stop asking our Teachers to do it (everything) for us, we might be ready to learn what it is they seek to teach us, which is that we already are what we look to them to teach us to be. See that, they say, and we will be them, and then some. Which ultimately is the Object of Life.

Don't seek it, be it.

REVELATIONS

When a sudden revelation comes, when we suddenly "see" it (it is so obvious), it is never from an effort of will. Instead, it comes in silence. It seems to "just be there." There is no cognitive process that precedes it. In fact, if there is, the revelation will not come.

Revelation is quiet, like cats' paws, soft, gentle, unobtrusive, and always it rings true. I imagine it to be a sort of parting of the veils, or a received whisper. It is what "Be Still, and know that I Am" is all about. Its most striking characteristic is that it is so obvious. Then its sweetness and simplicity follow. But it is always quiet. And because it comes through grace, all we can do is yield, wait and submit, and it will come. We cannot force it through any will or effort. All we can do is ask.

THE WAY HOME

In a general, albeit oversimplified, sort of way, these seem to be the steps we take along the spiritual path:

At first, we deny God vociferously and vehemently. "What I can't see, isn't."

Then, reluctantly, increasingly, we accept the possibility of God. "Well, I don't say yes, but I don't say no, either."

Until, tentatively, first suspiciously, then joyfully, we acknowledge the probability of God. "I have to admit there are some things I can't explain."

Finally, happily, even blissfully, we bask in the certainty of God. "Oh, God."

Until suddenly, spontaneously, dispassionately, there is none to affirm and nothing to deny. Only One, everywhere always, remarking, "Here I Am"

LOOK THIS WAY

The greater our dedication to God, the more evident is His dedication to us. It is in fact, of course, always maximal, but we see or experience it in our lives only to the degree of our commitment to Him. Thus, if we would choose to witness continuing evidence of God's active presence in our lives, we have only to choose to be continuously aware of Him, to claim Him as the principal focus of our lives.

In other words, look at what you want to see.

BORN AGAIN. AND AGAIN. AND AGAIN.

In a spiritual sense, one might observe that we are born three times, at least. Our first birth is into total and sole identification with and as the flesh. Here, so thoroughly identified are we with the body that at its inevitable death, we die, too. That is, we think we die. Convinced we are naught but the flesh, as we witness its demise, we convince ourselves of our own. Although we do, of course, continue - - (For however confused we may be on the subject, life is eternally eternal, with or without our concurrence!) - - we do not recognize that what continues is ourselves, so firmly do we believe ourselves to be dead. Thus, we live but we do not know that it is us. We carry with us through the physical death process no conscious recollection of having been before and of continuing to be. We assume ourselves to be another.

Our first rebirth or our second birth, then, is out of that I-am-the-body stage to identification with ourselves as a personality, the intangible aspect of the physical body which we ultimately call the soul. The soul as we see it at this point, of course, is still inexorably linked to the body, for here we believe that each body has a soul, and that there are therefore presumably as many souls as there are or ever were bodies. But the soul's destiny is not tied to the body's; at the body's death, the soul continues. Thus, having identified ourselves with the soul and not the flesh, we do not consider the latter's death to be our own. This time, we recognize ourselves as the being (the soul) which continues. We are still alive, and we know it. We have begun to understand the eternal nature of life.

From there, we are eventually born again beyond the limited, separative identity of "my" personality or soul which continues in time (albeit "forever") and in space (be it "in heaven" or some so-called astral plane, or even on earth, as posited by the belief in reincarnation), to an identity with or as the One (in the words of one who has, "The Father and I are One"). Here our sense of individual identity, of my self or soul as opposed to your self or soul, dies, and we are born again as the Universal which is Being Itself. Which I AM.

From the perspective of the I AM, of course, nothing has happened. From the perspective of the I AM, nothing ever happens. To whom would it happen? When? Where? The I AM simply is. The I AM is never born and therefore it never dies. Actually, we are not really ever born either; not once, twice, or even three times. It is only because we think we are that we are, and likewise that we die. Indeed, thinking and being are not the same thing; on this subject, Descartes was dead wrong. Or right, depending on who he thought he was! So long as he thinks he is Descartes or anyone else, he is. And so long as he thinks that that someone was born, he will be born, and, again, die. And be born again. And die again. Until he is what I AM ... which he is.

COMMITMENT AND SUFFERING

Along the way of spiritual unfoldment, there comes a time when we are asked to "lay it on the line", to "put up or shut up", to declare whether or not we mean business and are deadly serious in our choice to look upward instead of downward. It is at this moment that the "suffering" begins.

Until now, the spiritual "trip" was exciting, the discovery of new found things, the thrill of self-discovery. In fact, for many of us, it is the luster and the glamour, the promise of fun, that initially draw us to and get us started on the path in the first place. The fun involved in new ways of thinking and looking, the high derived from even small increments of newly acquired self-control that seem so mammoth in the beginning. It is all new teritory and, like taking a trip to foreign, unknown lands, that alone can be enough to recommend it!

But after a while, after we have been around a bit and the newness wears off, it all becomes commonplace. The luster seems to dull, the excitement to abate, the thrill to disappear. It becomes familiar and ordinary. It is at this very moment that our real growth begins. And it is here that many of us flounder and fall by the wayside.

It has been said that "many are called, few are chosen". I would reword that to say "many are called, few choose." Many begin the process, but few stick it out. Few of us have the perseverence, the commitment to struggle, the willingness to endure pain or to suffer the boredom that always attends the familiar. This is unfortunate, because that very sense of the familiar is the first sign-post that we are making progress, that the old habits we traded for new ones are gone, and the new practices are indeed becoming habits, a sign that we are learning. It is similar to the physical law which explains why the thrown projectile inevitably falls to earth after the initial impulse of energy that shot it up into the sky wanes. It is at this falling point that we need the greatest of energy to give a renewed impetus to the projectile, to maintain its speed and trajetory. And that requires effort, overcoming tedium, and certainly discomfort, to marshal the energy required to keep the projectile in flight against all natural law to bring it back to earth. This undertaking might even be the cause of considerable suffering! Particularly when we consider the enormous friction created by this effort, literally and figuratively.

One sign of our commitment is that we feel this suffering, this friction. By the word suffer, I do not necessarily mean wracking pain, or misery. There are all kinds of suffering. But I can say with certainty that if we are "comfortable", if we are easily content with things "as they are", then we are more than likely standing still, spiritually speaking. There are times to stand still, there are times to feel comfortable, but if this becomes our aim, if we wish to maintain this state at all costs, we have likely chosen to fall off the path of spiritual growth. So, by suffering I mean discomfort, a sense of stretching, a tension; and often, along with this, there is great joy, and moments of great exhilaration; times of immense delight with the world just as it is. This state of tension is experienced as a feeling of expansion, a pulling upward, a sense that we are much more than we seem. There can also be great physical and mental suffering along with this state. There are times when all seems dark and abysmal, when there seems to be no reason, no sense or direction in our life, when it all seems hopeless. And it is at these very times that we can be certain that we are making massive progress, for it is during these times that the greatest shedding of the old is taking place; that's <u>why</u> the discomfort and the suffering.

It is the greatest of indicators, this suffering, that things are changing, that we are in a state of grace, that God is with us. That state of grace is God°s helpful hand, His pushing and prodding, His aid in times of darkness that gets us from here to there. It is only the suffering of an uncomfortable, egocentric child that gives us evidence of the inner growth, the spiritual illumination that is taking place. How otherwise would we know that change was taking place, if there were not some childlike creature to inform us that the old was preferable to this new, unfamiliar, and <u>therefore</u> uncomfortable, state!?

Conversely, if there isn't discomfort (except of course in those of us who are greatly illuminated already - - and only each of us knows if the shoe fits!), then we must ask ourself, why isn't there? Or perhaps there is, and I am not being honest with myself? And if I am being honest with myself, why then do I not feel any change, any "suffering" in my spiritual life? Let us not forget that the greatest saints suffered greatly, both physically and/or mentally, but were continuously in a state of grace and in the palm of God's hand. Be certain, therefore, to discriminate between the comfort of the status quo and the ecstasy of a small glimpse into God. They are decidedly different, and if we are honest with ourself, we will see the difference.

Of course, the bottom line is the rewards gained through all this struggle. One of the greatest, and earliest, is freedom, the kind which most of us never even have an inkling of! This is the kind of freedom that God has, complete and dispassionate. It is more than worth all the struggle in the world!

"GOD, REVEAL THYSELF TO ME"
"YOU WHO?"

How long I had been asking God "to reveal Himself" to me, that, like the great saints, I may see Him in all life! Then, suddenly, it struck me: The body's eyes cannot see God because they see only an other, and God is not an other.

Consider the so-called human senses. Extraordinary as they are, the one thing they positively cannot experience or witness is themselves. My tongue can deliver to me the taste of virtually anything in the universe, except itself. However pleasing or offensive may be its odor, I cannot smell my own nose. My eyeballs, even should they possess the keenest vision in recorded medical history, cannot see themselves. To be sure, one might argue that I can feel myself, but I cannot feel the finger that is feeling, except with another finger. There is no way around it; the human sense organs, my personal witnesses and reporters, are hopelessly separative, eternally other-oriented. And God, the object of my search, is irrevocably not "an other"!

Now, what about the mind, where I do all my thinking? It is there that I actually experience the reports of my senses. Can the mind be any less inherently separative, or other-oriented, than the information it processes? Presumably not, for the mind is not really a thing or a place; the mind is simply the phenomenon of processing information or data, a phenomenon we call thinking. We say that thinking is a process which takes place "in the mind", but surely that is merely a manner of speaking. Clearly, thinking _is_ the mind. So, the mind is no more than its contents, or than the processing of its contents, and as they are limited, so is it. The mind cannot process what its witnesses cannot report. Thus, the mind can no more know God than the senses can find Him.

In this regard, consider the senses to be the servants of the mind, or perhaps better, of the mindset. That is, they see, hear, feel, taste, and smell what we believe. Our mindset, or our paradigm, describes or defines for us the way things are, and the function of the senses is to retrieve evidence to that effect, to prove the truth of what we have already determined. Thus, what is actually going on as ourselves may be the complete opposite of what we have been brought up to believe. It is not that things happen "out there" about which we gather data with our senses which we process in our minds and then react to accordingly. That is, we do not experience the events in our lives first and then reflect on them; if anything, it is the other way around. Thinking is prior to experiencing. Not necessarily in time, but in precedence. (Time, after all, even the physicists are now telling us, is an illusion hardly to be taken seriously.) Experience is not external and objective (as in, "seeing is believing"); experience is a function of prior thought. Can we go so far as to say that the mind thinks and the body (the ultimate experience, after all) is the evidence of that thought, of the thinking process itself? And that it is part of this "system" that it all shall seem to have happened the other way around?

Thus, to know God (to have Him revealed to me), I have to stop thinking; I have to cease looking for Him by the evidence of my senses, in my thoughts. But that is where I exist, isn't it, in my thoughts? Even the concept "that I exist" is a thought. The I that I think I am is, after all, basically a thought. If I stop thinking, what will happen to me? We have just said that thoughts create or precede experiences; if I cease thinking, I will cease experiencing. But experiences (or sense reports) are what confirm my existence. If I stop experiencing, I may forget (from lack of evidence) that I exist. Indeed, if I cease thinking (and thus experiencing), I may cease to exist in fact! And yet, cease to exist as what? Cease to exist as an object capable of witness by the senses; or, cease to exist as "an other". Remember we said that the senses are capable of witnessing or, if you will, sensing, only an other; if they cannot sense me (which, if I stop thinking they will not be able to do) I will presumably no longer be an other. I will be what God is.

So, God's answer to my whine, "Reveal Thyself to me," is, "Who are you?" For so long as I think God is an other to be revealed (don't I really mean experienced?), I cannot know Him. I cannot know Him not because He is hiding from me, but because the senses I use to find Him are specifically designed not to find Him. And that is so because the senses are the servant or function of the thought process, of which it is the overriding, all-consuming purpose to establish and continuously confirm our existence as an other! And evidence of God, the One Who Is and is no other, cannot but do irreparable harm to that. So, perhaps what God is really saying to me, as I pray that He make Himself evident to me, is, "Dearly beloved, stop thinking of Me"!

In the end, it comes to this: Who am I?
To which the answer is, Who's asking?

Solve that riddle, and, in the words of the Teacher, It is finished.

EAT A LION

The so-called savages would eat a lion or some other beast in order to gain its courage, strength, or other characteristics.

Similarly, seeing God all around us, in and as everything we perceive, we ingest Him in order to become Him. "This flesh is My Body, this wine My Blood."

Perhaps it is not so much that we become <u>what</u> we eat as it is that we become <u>why</u> we eat. Thus, "What are we eating?" might be better stated, "What are we feeding?" If we eat to sustain our bodies, we become (or continue as) those bodies. But if we eat to transform ourselves (to become something else, lions or God, as we might choose) then we will do so.

Once again, eating, like everything else in our lives, must become for us an act of meditation or prayer, another aspect of our continuing search and worship.

THIS I KNOW

Jesus can say to Pontius Pilate (as say all our Teachers to us who torment them), "I don't care what you think of me, because I know that in Truth you love me."

And he's right.

SPIRITUAL GROWTH AND ITS MANIFESTATIONS

Growth is often attended by anxiety. Just as this is true in the transformation from childhood to maturity called adolescence, so it is true of inner, spiritual growth. The cause of this anxiety is change, which growth is, and which generates the sense of fear of the "out there", the fear of responsibility, all the assumed fears that come with a change in consciousness from the known to the unknown. The difference is that the change is spiritual, not physical, even though the symptoms will likely manifest, or be felt, physically.

Can you remember your own adolescence? If it was difficult, this will probably be just as difficult.

DISENGAGEMENT

If it is true that the body is simply a means or a vehicle for God to see and witness His Universe as me or through me, then the ability to disengage from this body of mine should be just as easy for me to do as it is to disengage from the bodies of others, which I do automatically. In other words, if I can look on and watch an animal in pain without actually feeling its pain, which all of us can do, and do do, then I should be able to do exactly the same thing with regard to my own pain and my own body; if, that is, I truly believe or know that my body is simply a vehicle for God's experience, and is not actually me or mine!

ALL ABOUT BEING HONEST

We cannot even begin to grow spiritually if we are not fully committed to being honest with ourselves and the world. The importance of honesty within is absolutely paramount and cannot be stressed enough.

We are taught to lie by our society, our families, and our teachers, and from the moment we begin to understand and use words, we spend most of the rest of our lives lying in one way or another. We profess to honesty when we tell others of their perceived failings, but is this honesty, or is it simply ego aggrandizement at their expense? We profess to honesty when we "let it all hang out", when we insist on "expressing ourselves" regardless of the effect on others, but is this honesty, or is it the behavior of a spoiled child, self-indulgently insisting on having its own way, that the world "accept me as I am"? We proselytize the "unsaved", the so-called lost souls of the earth, whether or not they ask for it, in the name of honesty, but is this honesty, or is it self-righteousness, the petty conviction that "we have found the answer" and, therefore, obviously they have not. Do we consider our actions, our thoughts, our motives, or do we just react impulsively, make a loud noise and create a commotion on the excuse that we are "doing my thing".

There is in fact an "external" Truth, a Truth of the Universe which is true in every manifestation and expression, but we will not see or know it so long as we are mired in the hypocritical falsehoods and empty moralities of our separative world. The only way out of this trap is through stark, disciplined (and I stress the word disciplined), and continuous censorship of our every thought and action. How can we do this? How can we monitor and check the lier we have become? Perhaps the best way is to find a friend or a teacher who is willing to work with us, to help keep us honest. Of course, to be effective, this friend must be equally committed to being honest himself, and more concerned about growth, ours and his, than "happiness and comfort", ours and his. Also, he must be willing to bear our resentment, for sometimes, and in some cases often!, his help may come to us painfully and or embarrassingly, and we aren't going to like it. Finding such a friend is not easy for they are not common, but when we do, we will "recognize" him. We will know his love for us, and we will always come away from him stronger, surer, perhaps unsettled and maybe even angry, but invariably wiser. We should not be surprised if this friend is not the "master" or "guru" we might expect but rather a colleague, an associate, a peer, perhaps even a spouse. It doesn't matter just who he (or she) turns out to be, for ultimately we are taught by everyone and everything; if we are truly committed to learning and to growth, a puppy chasing a squirrel can lead us to the Truth as well as Christ on the cross. After all, the Teacher is within; the external event or personality is just a pointer, or a prod.

Giving up the lying habit is extraordinarily difficult. We are too well trained in it. Success requires a deep seated, life-long commitment, a decision to seek the Truth at all costs, no matter what. And, predictably, even this commitment can be turned into a lie, as we fashion our own spiritual journey into an excuse for comparing, judging, and condemning others, always and only to make ourselves feel "better". It is a tricky business, learning honesty, and a continuous struggle, but it can be won, with God's help - - which, if we mean it, He will provide.

REASONS FOR GURUS OR SPIRITUAL TEACHERS

The main reason to go to a guru, or a spiritual Teacher, is not so much to <u>learn</u> from him or her, but to <u>see</u> God, or a "reasonable facsimile thereof". (Of course, how closely the facsimile resembles the "real McCoy" depends on the clarity or purity of the viewer.) We long to "see God", to "touch" Him, to be with Him, and while we know that He is all pervasive, and that we cannot actually physically see Him (so long as we are looking for a separate Him), there is the human need to see and touch Him, sensually. The fully enlightened teacher is <u>That</u>, just as Jesus is That. He or she fills that need for us in response to our demand. Their only purpose is to <u>be</u> there, to fill our need to touch! And that is the primary reason to be in their company, to fill that need. The learning and practice can, and must be, done apart, by oneself, between oneself and God. But the longing to <u>see</u> God, to touch God, can properly be filled by the physical presence of a God-filled Teacher.

PLEASE, DON'T AWAKEN ME WHEN I'M SLEEPING!

Virtually all of the Teachers tell us that it is not their intention to make our lives comfortable, but to disrupt them. They come, they tell us, to awaken us, not to fluff up our pillows. At this, everyone of us nods dutifully, and then screams bloody murder at the first prick of discomfort.

Think about it. We curse "the enemy" whenever we feel our lives being the least bit shaken, and we "praise the Lord" for every slumberful moment of uninterrupted routine. Even as we have been specifically alerted that the Truth is likely to come to us the other way around.

Consider it this way. It is the function of an alarm clock to awaken a sleeper, and it does so by being irritating. If it is not just a little bit irritating at least, an alarm clock will never awaken anyone. And the deeper the sleep, the greater the irritation necessary to awaken. The Teachers tell us we are asleep. Thus, we must expect to find them at least just a little bit irritating. Indeed, if we do not find them so, chances are we are not yet hearing them.

Ultimately, it is all about change, and our resistance to change. Change is by definition disruptive. And, God knows, there is no less welcome change than awakening from sleep, especially awakening abruptly from deep sleep.

Consider this.
 I love you.
Which is the same as saying,
 I love God.
Which is the same as saying,
 God loves you.
Which is the same as saying,
 God loves God.
Which is the same as saying,
 God Gods God.
Which is the same as saying,
 God.
Which is all there is.

WHO WROTE WHAT

For those readers interested in knowing who of us wrote which of the entries in the book, the following information is provided.

Material from Nancy's journals appears on pages 1, 4, 10, 11, 14, 15, 18, 19, 24-27, 30-32, 38, 42-45, 48, 51-54, 59, 60, 65-67, 70-77, 79, 80, 84, 89, 92, 93, 96, 100-102, 107-110.

Material from Stefan's journals appears on pages 2, 3, 5-9, 12, 13, 16, 17, 20-23, 28, 29, 33-37, 39-41, 46, 47, 49, 50, 55-58, 61-64, 68, 69, 78, 81-83, 85-88, 90, 91, 94, 95, 97-99, 103-106, 111, 112.